Walking the Path of Faith

A Companion Volume to
Planting Seeds of Faith

Walking the Path of Faith

More Fun Character-building Activities for LDS Children

CEDAR FORT

A Companion Volume to

Planting Seeds of Faith

Alison Palmer

Second Printing: July, 2004

International Standard Book Number
0-88290-764-6

Horizon Publishers' Catalog and Order Number
H2106

Printed and distributed
in the United States of America by

CEDAR FORT

Address:
925 North Main Street
Springville, Utah 84664

Phone:
Local Phone: (801) 489-4084
WATS (toll free): 1 (800) SKYBOOK
FAX: (800) 489-1097

Internet:
Website: http://www.horizonpublishersbooks.com

Acknowledgments

The Author wishes to thank Jennifer Beckett and George Hemingway for their hard work creating the illustrations included in this book.

Appreciation also is expressed to Duane and Jean Crowther, senior editors at Horizon Publishers, and to Sam Richardson and Jenny Beckstead, who typeset and proof-read the book.

Table of Contents

MY GOSPEL STANDARDS

I will follow Heavenly Father's plan for me.
I will remember my baptismal covenant and listen to the Holy Ghost.
I will choose the right. I know I can repent when I make a mistake.
I will be honest with Heavenly Father, others, and myself.
I will use the names of Heavenly Father and Jesus Christ reverently. I will not swear or use crude words.
I will do those things on the Sabbath that will help me feel close to Heavenly Father and Jesus Christ.
I will honor my parents and do my part to strengthen my family.
I will keep my mind and body sacred and pure, and I will not partake of things that are harmful to me.
I will dress modestly to show respect for Heavenly Father and myself.
I will only read and watch things that are pleasing to Heavenly Father.
I will only listen to music that is pleasing to Heavenly Father.
I will seek good friends and treat others kindly.
I will live now to be worthy to go to the temple, serve a mission, and do my part to have an eternal family.

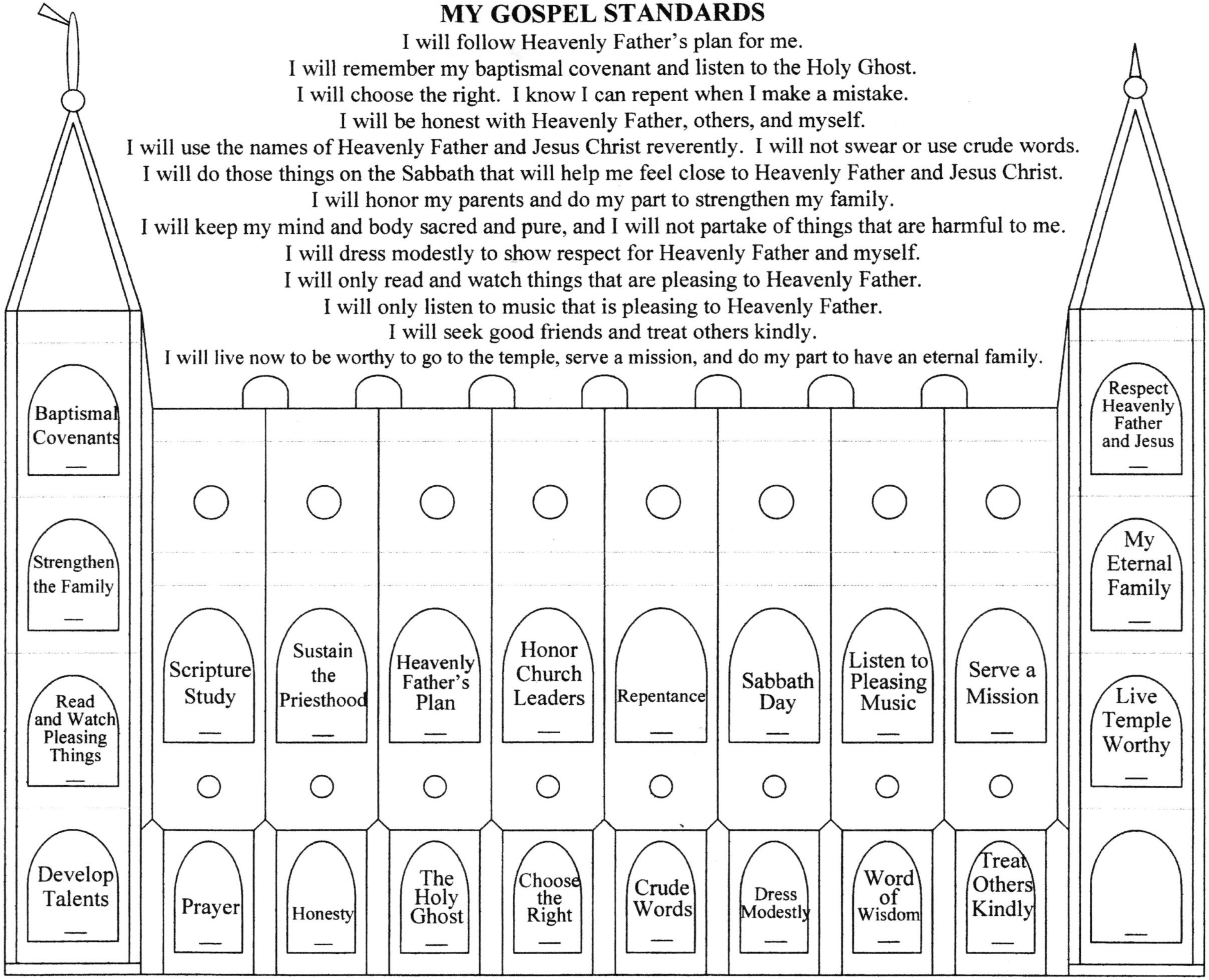

•The outer picture lists the basic themes to be covered and allows a place to number them for order of coverage during the year.
•The inside windows give the title of a corresponding lesson from this book and a place to list the date it was taught.
•Blank windows are included for customization.
•You may also may a copy of the diagram, block out the words and re-copy it allowing you to completely customize your calendar.

Instructions:

•Copy both pages onto cardstock paper.
•Color the outer picture and number the topics in order to be covered.
•Use a hobby knife to cut the 24 windows on their curved lines only, leave the flat lines intact.
•Place the temple picture on top of lesson sheet and verify placement before gluing in place.

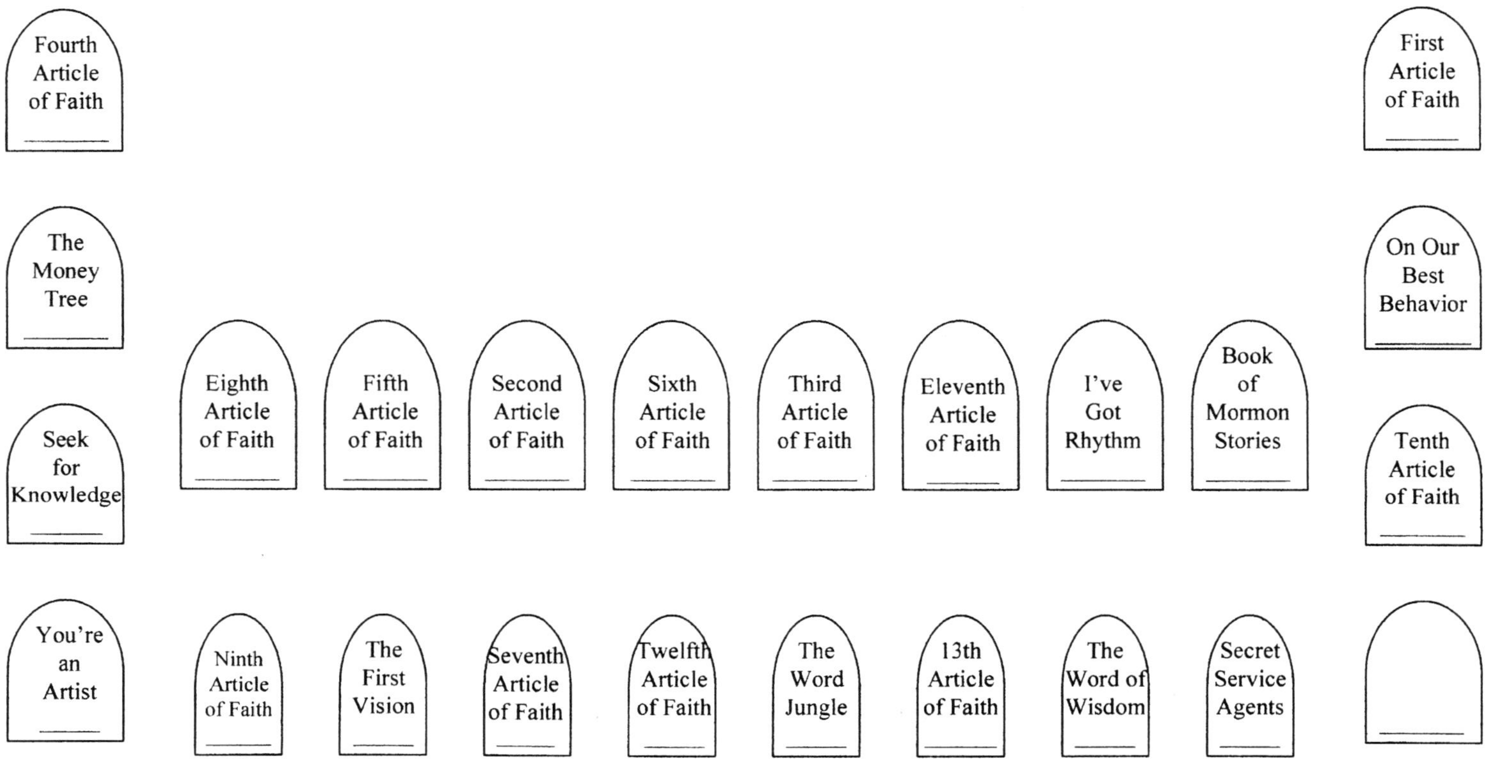

One
The First Article of Faith

Scripture: "The Father has a body of flesh and bones as tangible as man's; the Son also; but the Holy Ghost has not a body of flesh and bones, but is a personage of Spirit. Were it not so, the Holy Ghost could not dwell in us."

—D&C 130:22

Song: "When Jesus Christ was Baptized," *Children's Songbook*, pg. 102 or "The First Article of Faith," *Children's Songbook*, pg. 122.

Treat: Triangle-shaped finger sandwiches

Lesson:
Materials Needed:
* Chalkboard and Chalk
* A clear glass filled with water
* Gospel art picture #403 "The First Vision"

Write the First Article of Faith on the chalkboard. Draw a triangle underneath.

Show the children the glass of water and ask them what it is. Tell the children that in some ways, it is easy to tell what the glass holds. But in other ways, it is difficult. Many years ago if you would have told someone that the glass held millions and millions of little pieces that were stuck together in groups of three; no one would have believed you. Today in science we know that this is true. Water is made of chemical or element building blocks. It takes three atoms (or elements), two that are hydrogen and one that is oxygen, to stick together and make a molecule of water. Ask the children if they believe that this true, even though they can't see all the little pieces that make a glass of water.

Once, Joseph Smith was asked to write down everything that our church believed. What he wrote was published in a newspaper and can be found in our scriptures today. He wrote thirteen statements that we call The Articles of Faith.

The first statement he wrote was meant to help people understand what we knew about Heavenly Father and the other members of what is known as the Godhead. Many religions don't really understand who or what Heavenly Father is. Some think He is just a spirit. Some think He is the same person as Jesus Christ. Some feel He is so different from us that we shouldn't even try to understand Him.

Have the children read the First Article of Faith out loud with you.

Show the picture of the first vision.

Ask the children what is happening in the picture. Allow them to share their responses, remind them that the whole reason Joseph Smith went to the grove to pray was because he was confused about the different churches and what they believed.

Hint to them that he learned something very important even before he asked which church to join. Remind them of what you have been discussing and help them to see that the very first thing Joseph learned was what Heavenly Father and Jesus are really like.

Remind them of the different beliefs you mentioned. Ask them if they feel that God is just a spirit with no form or shape, or if he is the same person as Jesus. List their true answers about Heavenly Father on the board.

Then, expand the discussion. Help the children brainstorm everything that they do know about the members of the Godhead. Make sure they include bodies of flesh and bone and bodies of spirit appropriately. They should also include things about their nature, loving and kind, all knowing, as well as their responsibilities, literal father of us all, creator, savior, comforter and guide. Try to help them paint a very clear picture.

After they have exhausted their lists, direct their attention to the triangle you drew. Label each of the sides with a member of the Godhead and write the word Godhead in the middle. Tell the children that one of the easiest ways for people to get confused about Heavenly Father, Jesus, and the Holy Ghost is by misunderstanding the scriptures. There are lots of places where is says that Heavenly Father and Jesus are "one."

It can get confusing, just like looking at a glass of water and not understanding its parts. If the atoms didn't work together, or have the same purpose, you wouldn't get water at all. If one side of the triangle you drew was missing, the other two sides would collapse. The members of the Godhead are all separate people, but they all work toward the same goal. The thing that they want most, and that they cooperate on completely is us. They want us to be able to return and live with them again. Working together to help us learn and grow is what makes them "one," or the Godhead.

Testify of the truthfulness of this principle to the children. Emphasize how the spirit has helped you come to know more about your Savior and Heavenly Father. Help them recognize the feelings from the presence of spirit during your discussion. Express to them your gratitude for this knowledge and how it helps you want to be closer to your Heavenly Father.

Gently remind them that though you have used several names for each of the deity in your discussion, it was done in the presence of the spirit and in respect for who they are. Discourage them from using these names in every day language or exposing themselves to uses of these words in crude or non-religious tones. When we do this, we are forgetting how important they really are to us, and how much they love us. It is hurtful to them and disrespectful of us.

Help the children begin the memorization process by holding up one finger as you describe each member of the Godhead as stated in the First Article of Faith. Emphasize the accompanying descriptions of the nature of Father and Son. Have the children repeat it with you, counting them off on their own fingers several times. Many will be ready to pass the First Article of Faith off at this point, encourage them all to go home and practice sharing the truths they've learned and the Article of Faith with their families.

Activity:

Materials Needed:

* Fabric ties
* Large playing area

Have the children run three-legged races to emphasize three working as one for a universal purpose.

Use this lesson to re-enforce:

* *Faith in God*, general requirements
* *Primary 5*, lesson 36
* *Gospel Principles*, "The Articles of Faith"
* *My Gospel Standards*

Two
The Second Article of Faith

Scripture: "And in that day the Holy Ghost fell upon Adam, which beareth record of the Father and the Son, saying: I am the Only Begotten of the Father from the beginning, henceforth and forever, that as thou hast fallen thou mayest be redeemed, and all mankind, even as many as will. And in that day Adam blessed God and was filled, and began to prophesy concerning all the families of the earth, saying: Blessed be the name of God, for because of my transgression my eyes are opened, and in this life I shall have joy, and again in the flesh I shall see God."

—Moses 5:9-10

Song: "I Lived in Heaven," *Children's Songbook*, pg. 4 or "The Second Article of Faith," *Children's Songbook*, pg. 122.

Treat: Baked Apples

Lesson:
Materials Needed:
* Copy of the included illustrations, colored and cut
* Chalkboard or other area for display of the story pieces
* Tape
* Television and video player
* *Family Home Evening Video Supplement set* to "The Pump" (9 minutes)
* Copies of the section "Agency and Accountability" from the church produced pamphlet *For the Strength of Youth,* 2001

Be familiar with the story found in Moses 4.

Pass out the pieces to the story of the Garden of Eden to the children. Have them help you assemble the picture while you review the story of Adam and the fall.

As you tell the story, remind the children that the garden was a perfect place to live and that everything was provided for Adam and Eve. They had a choice to make. They knew why they had been sent to earth and they knew the rules Heavenly Father had given them. Did the rules allow them to do everything that they were given bodies to do? Allow the children to express their own opinions on what their own choices would have been.

Because of the choices Adam and Eve made, we have our free agency today to make lots of choices. But, Adam did break a rule to give us this gift. What happened to him because he broke a rule? What happens to each of us if we break a rule?

Would it be fair for us to be punished for something we didn't do? Give the children a few examples that they can relate with and let them choose their own judgment or punishment. Read the Second Article of Faith to the children. Tell them that they need to remember three key words in this statement. The words are: punished, sins, and transgressions. Ask them to repeat the words with you several times then share their views on what they think the words mean. Correct any misconceptions they might have.

Each of us needs to learn to take responsibility for our own actions. This is the way Heavenly Father expects us to be. We are here to learn and grow, and part of that is making mistakes and repenting. Part of it is also doing things right and being blessed for it. Each of us must do this for ourselves. It wouldn't be fair if we had to repent because our neighbor was mean to his dog. It also wouldn't be fair if everyone got to go to the temple because their bishop was worthy, not them.

Show the video, and then have several of the children take turns reading portions of the statement on accountability from For the Strength of Youth out loud for the group. Allow them to express their opinions about what they read and saw.

Then, ask them if they can remember the three key words from The Second Article of Faith. Have them review these words several more times than put them back into the context of the entire statement. Memorization should be well begun as this point. Encourage them to continue practicing until they can pass off this Article of Faith.

Activity:

Materials Needed:

* Index Cards
* Envelopes with holes punched in one end
* Large skein of yarn
* Scissors
* Marking pen
* Tape

Write the choices and consequences listed below on the index cards, or make up your own situations that you feel are appropriate for your children.

Place the cards inside of the envelopes, label the choice with a number and the letter "a", and label the corresponding consequence with the same number and the letter "b". Seal the envelopes. Use the hole punch to create a hole in one end of each envelope (be sure to avoid the index card inside).

Cut a piece of yarn at least 30 feet long. Tie one end to an "a" envelope and the other end to the corresponding "b" envelope, using the holes in the envelopes as anchors. Wrap the yarn up around the "b" envelope. Secure the "a" envelopes to a stationary object (table or chair, etc.) in the classroom. Repeat this process with all the envelopes.

Now string the various yarns over and around all of the room where your lesson will be held, only leave the area you will need to conduct the lesson uncovered.

After the lesson is complete instruct the children to choose an "a" envelope from the table or central location where you placed them. They must then follow the path of their string and de-tangle it from everyone else's choices to find their consequences.

Once everyone had gotten their yarn untangled and found their "b" envelope, have them take turns reading their choice and its results.

The game can be repeated multiple times by having the children re-string the maze, trade cards with a partner and find their way out again. Do not use this method for the initial game however as it negates reinforcing that we can not be judged for someone else's actions.

* ***Choice***—You found your mom's stash of cookies and ate them all.
Consequence—Now you have a stomach ache.

* ***Choice***—Father asked you to clean out the garage before he gets home from work and you do it.
Consequence—He was looking for the target for your compound bow, since you cleaned out the garage, he was able to find it and you can practice together.

* ***Choice***—You decided you didn't want to go to church today.
Consequence—Your friend called later to tell you about the awesome game your teacher had for an object lesson, you were sorry you missed it.

* ***Choice***—You studied for your geography test.
Consequence—You aced the test and got to celebrate by going out for pizza.

* ***Choice***—You didn't read your scriptures this week.
Consequence—When a friend tries to tempt you to do something you shouldn't, you find it's harder to say "no" than it usually is.

* ***Choice***—If you pay your tithing you won't have enough money to buy the new CD you want, but you paid it any way.
Consequence—Your mom saw the CD on sale and bought it for you as a gift.

* ***Choice***—Your mom asks you to take treats to the new family on your street.
Consequence—You discover that they have a child just your age that seems shy but nice.

* ***Choice***—You found some money in the locker room at school. No one knew who it belonged to so you decided to keep it.
Consequence—Now you're spending all your time worrying about getting caught and somebody wanting their money back.

* ***Choice***—You decide to play with you little brother, even though he's always a pain.
Consequence—It seems that since you took time to play with him, he doesn't bug you as much.

* ***Choice***—You decided to dye your hair purple.
Consequence—The dye didn't work right, now instead of looking cool, you look like one of your mom's sick eggplants.

* ***Choice***—You buy a shirt that is a little immodest, but if you hold your arms right no one can tell.

Consequence—Your friend says the shirt would look cool with a pair of shorts that is definitely not appropriate, but she's right and you buy them, too. Now you have a whole outfit you have to hide from your parents.

Use this lesson to re-enforce:

* *Faith in God*, general requirements
* Cub Scouts, Wolf advancement 12, Bear advancement 24
* *My Gospel Standards*
* *Gospel Principles*, "The Articles of Faith"
* *Family Home Evening Resource Book*, lesson 8
* *For the Strength of Youth*, "agency and accountability"
* *Primary 3*, lesson 27
* *Primary 4*, lessons 23 and 24
* *Old Testament Gospel Doctrine Manual*, lesson 4

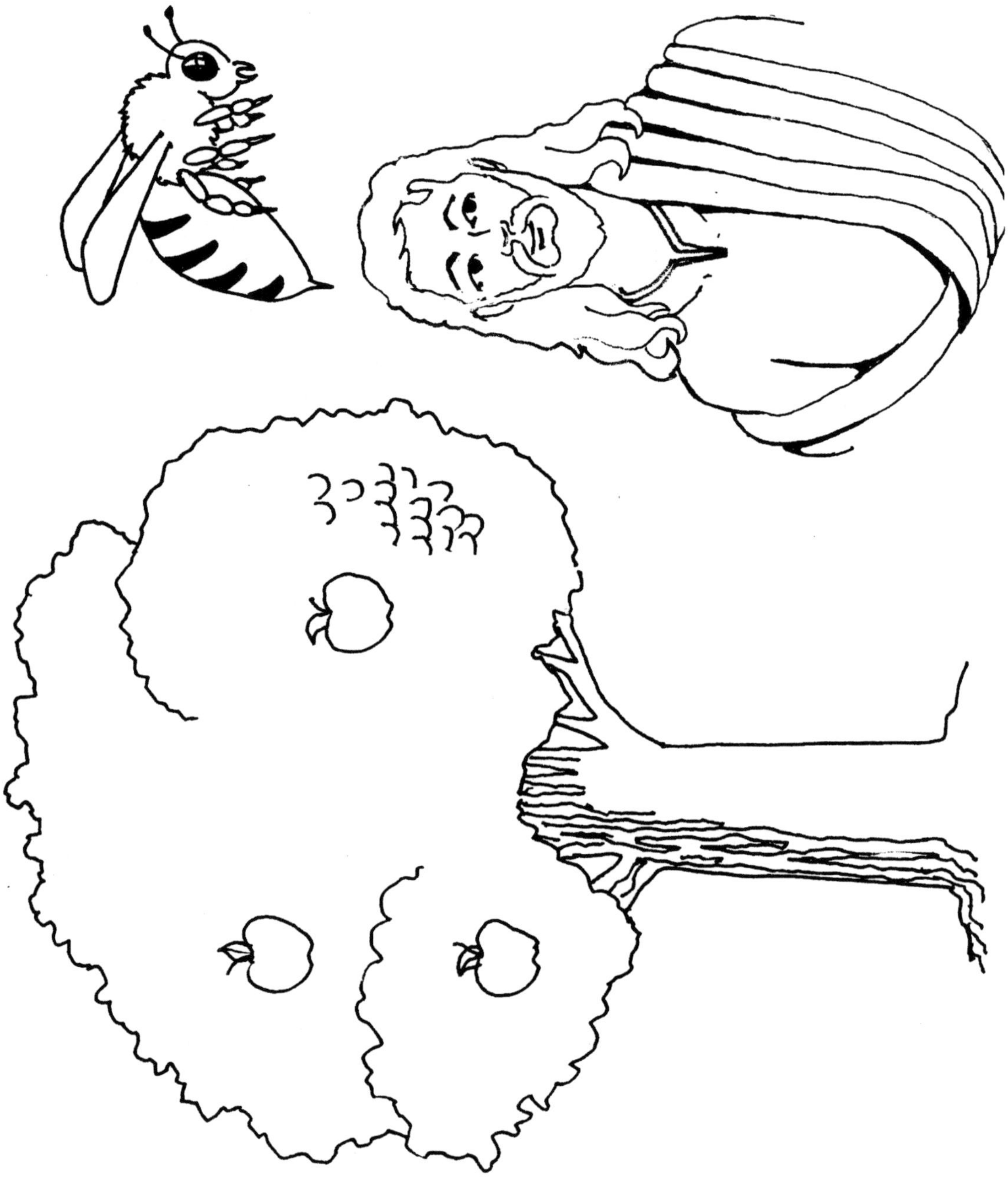

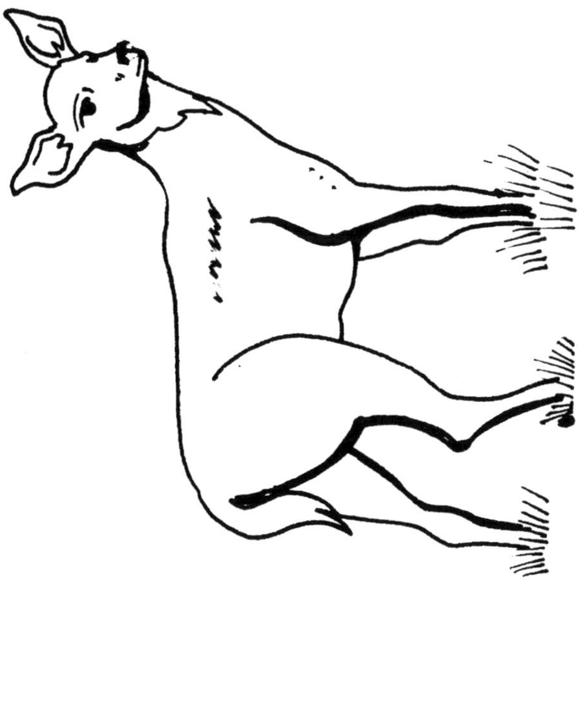

Three
The Third Article of Faith

Scripture: "For, said he, I have repented of my sins, and have been redeemed of the Lord; behold I am born of the Spirit. And the Lord said unto me: Marvel not that all mankind, yea, men and women, all nations, kindreds, tongues and people, must be born again; yea, born of God, changed from their carnal and fallen state, to a state of righteousness, being redeemed of God, becoming his sons and daughters;"

—Mosiah 27:24-26

Song: "Help Me, Dear Father," *Children's Songbook*, pg. 99 or "The Third Article of Faith," *Children's Songbook*, pg. 123.

Treat: Scarlet and Snow dessert-strawberries and whipped cream

Lesson:
Materials Needed:
* Television and video player
* Church produced video "The Lamb of God" (27 minutes)
* Copies of the section "Repentance" from the church produced pamphlet *For the Strength of Youth*, 2001
* Large index cards and writing utensils for each child

Begin this lesson with your testimony. Share your feelings about the gospel and Savior briefly with the children. You want to create a peaceful and reverent environment conducive to the spirit.

Show "The Lamb of God."

Ask the children to share the feelings they experienced while watching the video. To help them recognize the spirit, also share your own feelings and the sensations associated with the spirit.

Have them convey the basic story line of what they just saw, then ask them why this all needed to happen.

Share in your own words, and as prompted by the spirit, why these events were so important to each of us. Then introduce them to the Third Article of Faith.

Help them understand that what they just witnessed being depicted in the movie was our Savior's atonement for our sins. It was a cleansing and washing away of all of our mistakes and shortcomings so that we could have a chance to be perfect. Only if we can overcome those things, with the Savior's help, can we return to live with Him and Heavenly Father after we die. That is what being "saved" means. Emphasize that the atonement can only work if we are trying our best to live as Jesus would have us live, and exercising the gift of repentance that he has given us.

Read about "Repentance" from the pamphlet and testify of the truthfulness of the things you have read.

Have the children write the words of this Article of Faith down on their index cards, encourage them to take this home and place it somewhere that they can see and study it each day.

Choose one of the experiments, listed below, to help illustrate your discussion with the youth on the effects of sin and repentance. Do the experiment at this time to re-emphasize the importance of repentance and a savior to help us beyond ways that we can help ourselves. He atones for our sins and washes them away entirely. Share Isaiah 1:18 with them, then invite them to experience the affects of the atonement for themselves both literally in the prepared activities and spiritually as they ask for forgiveness of their own sins and resolve to do better each day of their lives.

Activity:

Materials Needed:

Each activity and its needed materials are listed separately. Make sure you have enough materials for an experiment to be executed several times, also secure typed or written instructions at each station so that the children can operate with independence. Set up your teaching area into stations and allow the children to cycle through several experiments and draw their own conclusions about the process and how it represents the effects of sin and repentance in our lives.

Note: Have the children wear old clothes that can be stained and spilled on. Plan on conducting the experiments outside or provide protective coverings for the tables and floor. Emphasize to the children that none of the mixtures you will be making are for consumption.

Experiment #1:

* Clear plastic cup
* 1/2 cup water
* 1 small bottle of phenol red (pool test chemical)
* 1/2 tsp baking soda
* 1/4 cup white vinegar
* Spoon

Place the water in the cup, and add 3 drops of phenol red. The water will turn slightly pink.

Add baking soda, stir. Water will turn bright red.

Add vinegar. Solution will bubble, when bubbles settle, water will be only tinted slightly yellow.

Adding more baking soda will bring back the pink.

More vinegar will take the color back out.

Experiment #2:
* Clear plastic cup
* Food coloring, any color
* 1/2 cup of water
* 1/4 cup of bleach

Place water in the cup. Add 2-3 drops of food coloring (bright colors work best). Swirl the cup around gently to distribute the color evenly.

Add the bleach to the mixture, and once again swirl the cup gently. It will take a few seconds but the color will disappear. It leaves behind a slightly yellow-tinged liquid.

A few more drops of color can be added. They will disperse then slowly fade again.

Experiment #3:
* Blank paper
* Paintbrush
* 3 clear plastic cups
* 1/2 cup water
* 1/2 tsp. Flour
* 1/4 cup water
* 3-5 drops of iodine
* Lemon juice
* Spoon

Mix 1/2 cup water with flour.

Use paintbrush to write a message or word on the paper. Set it aside to dry.

Rinse paintbrush for further use.

When dry, mix 1/4 cup of water with a few drops of iodine till the water slightly browns.

Use the paintbrush to apply the iodine mixture over the paper and previously written word. Paper will turn blue-purple and words will be visible.

Rinse paintbrush for further use.

Apply lemon juice to message and set aside to dry. The message should disappear again in approximately five minutes.

Experiment #4:
* Several dull, corroded pennies
* Small paper plates
* Table salt
* Vinegar
* Straw
* Plastic cup
* Small amount of water

Place a penny in the middle of a plate.

Sprinkle a thin layer of salt over the penny.

Use the straw and your finger as a vacuum to draw up a small amount of vinegar. Carefully drop the vinegar onto the penny.

Allow substance to bubble. When it is finished, rinse the penny off in the cup of water. Repeat the process with the other side of the penny.

Use this lesson to re-enforce:

* *Faith in God*, general requirements
* *Gospel Principles*, "The Articles of Faith" and chapter 23
* *For the Strength of Youth*, "Repentance"
* *My Gospel Standards*
* *Family Home Evening Resource Book*, lesson 10
* *Primary 1*, lesson 40
* *Primary 2*, lesson 41
* *Primary 3*, lessons 32 and 33
* *Primary 6*, lesson 5
* *Primary 7*, lesson 30
* *New Testament Gospel Doctrine Manual*, lesson 23
* *Doctrine and Covenants Gospel Doctrine Manual*, lesson 16
* *Aaronic Priesthood 1*, lesson 35
* *Young Women 2*, lesson 26

Four
The Fourth Article of Faith

Scripture: "And he commandeth all men that they must repent, and be baptized in his name, having perfect faith in the Holy One of Israel, or they cannot be saved in the kingdom of God."

—2 Nephi 9:23

Song: "I Like My Birthdays," *Children's Songbook*, pg. 104 or "The Fourth Article of Faith," *Children's Songbook*, pg. 124.

Treat: Things that can be served in fours—apple and orange slices, grapes, snack mix with four ingredients, sandwiches in four sections.

Lesson:
Materials needed:
* Pencils for each child
* Copies of the "Fourth Article of Faith Match-up" for each child

Ask the children if they can guess what the Fourth Article of Faith talks about. Allow the children to give their ideas. Praise the children who give correct answers and assure all the children that there is an easy way to remember what number four is about. It lists four important things we need to do to get back to Heavenly Father.

These four things are called the "first principles and ordinances of the gospel."

To help the children learn what these and other terms from this Article of Faith mean, help them complete the definition match page as you discuss each portion of this statement.

After each section is reviewed help the children repeat the Article of Faith from the beginning through what has been learned so far. By the end of the discussion each child should be familiar enough with the Article of Faith to begin passing it off from memory.

Answer Key:

1. I
2. J
3. B
4. D
5. F
6. A
7. H
8. E
9. G
10. C

Activity:

Materials needed:

* Roll of masking tape (if playing inside)
* Piece of sidewalk chalk (if playing outside)
* Large clear area for play
* Rubber bouncing ball

Key Words:

1. Faith
2. Repentance
3. Baptism
4. Holy Ghost

Play the following version of "Four Square."

Mark off a large square (at least 12' by 12') then divide it into 4 smaller squares.

Each square is assigned a number 1-4 and its key word, and then a child stands outside each square.

The child at square one begins play by calling out a number and corresponding key word then bouncing the ball in that square for the child to catch.

That child repeats the process by calling out a new number and word and bouncing it to that child. Any number can be chosen but they must use the correct key word. If the correct key word is not used, that player forfeits his turn and play starts again with the previous player.

For large groups simply assemble more squares.

For groups larger than four but smaller than eight: four begin play, if a wrong word is called out or a player fails to catch a ball bounced into their square they are out and replaced by another child from the sidelines. Play continues until all the children have been able to play.

Use this lesson to re-enforce:

* *Faith in God*, general requirements
* *Gospel Principles*, "The Articles of Faith"
* *Family Home Evening Resource Book*, lesson 13
* *Primary 3*, lesson 12
* *Primary 7*, lesson 6
* *Aaronic Priesthood 1*, lesson 5
* *Aaronic Priesthood 2*, lesson 3

Fourth Article of Faith Match-Up

1. ______ Principle
2. ______ Ordinance
3. ______ Faith
4. ______ Repentance
5. ______ Baptism
6. ______ Immersion
7. ______ Remission
8. ______ Confirmation
9. ______ Gift
10. ______ Holy Ghost

A. To go completely under water.

B. Believing in something you can't see

C. The member of the Godhead who is a spirit

D. Changing your actions and attitude so that it more closely matches what Heavenly Father wants you to be like.

E. When a Melchizedek Priesthood holder lays his hands on a person's head to give the gift of the Holy Ghost and completes their membership into The Church of Jesus Christ of Latter-day Saints.

F. Going into the water with a Priesthood holder to show our willingness to follow Christ and become a member of His church.

G. A presentation of something to another person without concern for payment

H. To change a condition so that it no longer exists.

I. A fundamental law or rule.

J. An essential covenant we make with Heavenly Father so we can return to Him.

Five

The Fifth Article of Faith

Scripture: "Every elder, priest, teacher, or deacon is to be ordained according to the gifts and callings of God unto him; and he is to be ordained by the power of the Holy Ghost, which is in the one who ordains him."

—D&C 20:60

Song: "The Priesthood Is Restored," *Children's Songbook,* pg. 89 or "The Fifth Article of Faith," *Children's Songbook,* pg. 125.

Treat: "Key" lime pie

Lesson:

Materials Needed:

* Invite someone you know to come share a special family heirloom with the children, or
* Visit your local library for a copy of *Grandfather's Gold Watch* by Louise Garff Hubbard or other book about a family heirloom
* Gospel art picture #408 "Melchizedek Priesthood Restoration"
* Chalk and Chalkboard or Dry-erase board and marker
* Copy, color and cut the key visual aids
* Tape

Write the words to the Fifth Article of Faith on the chalkboard, do not include the words available on the key prompts but leave large spaces for the key prompts to be placed. Secure the keys to the bottom of the board.

Invite your guest to share the special value of having something that was a gift from someone important to you. How do you take care of it, what does it mean to you to have it, how does it help you remember the person who gave it to you?

After sharing the heirloom, or book, with the children, make a point of "forgetting" something from your car. Ask one of the children to go get it. Have the car locked, but do not give the child the key when you send them out. When they come back unsuccessful, send them out again with your car key.

When they return, ask the children what would have happened if you had sent them with the wrong key, or didn't have a key at all.

Express that there is something very special that Heavenly Father has given us. It is like a key that opens up wonderful gifts and blessings. It is passed from person to person, but only to those who will try their best to take care of it.

Allow them to guess what this key might be.

Show them the gospel art picture and prompt them in telling you what the picture depicts. Assure them that the priesthood power is the wonderful key that Heavenly Father blesses us with. It can only be given by Heavenly Father, through those who already hold the priesthood, and will only be given to those who are worthy of it and will try to honor it.

This special key allows a worthy holder to act in Heavenly Father's name, when he is prompted to do so through the spirit. Ask them to share with you how this gift is given and what it can do.

Read through the Article of Faith in its entirety. Explain that this statement tells of the need for Heavenly Father's authority to be in place when his work is done. A man must be ordained by the laying on of hands before they can do Heavenly Father's work.

Help the children place the keys into their proper place in the article of faith.

Slowly erase the surrounding words, repeating the Article of Faith with the children until all the words are gone except the keys.

Activity:

Materials Needed:

* One key

Play "Who has the key?"

Have the children stand in a circle with their hands behind their backs. Choose one child to stand in the middle as "it" and another child to be the "authority keeper." The "keeper" circles around the outside of the children and pretends to pass the key to each of them in turn and discretely passing the key to one child. Everyone is to act as if they have the key; the child in the middle has to guess who really has the key. When a child's name is called they must show whether or not they hold the true key. When the key is found, that child becomes "it" and the child who just finished being "it" becomes the "keeper," the old keeper takes a place in the circle.

Use this lesson to re-enforce:

* *Faith in God*, general requirements and "Preparing for the Priesthood"
* *Gospel Principles*, "The Articles of Faith" chapters 3 and 17
* *Family Home Evening Resource Book*, lesson 30
* *Primary 3*, lesson 9
* *Primary 5*, lessons 8, 17, 36 and 47
* *Primary 6*, lesson 33
* *Primary 7*, lesson 15
* *Doctrine and Covenants and Church History Gospel Doctrine Manual*, lessons 8 and 25
* *Aaronic Priesthood 1*, lesson 37
* *Aaronic Priesthood 3*, lesson 49
* *Young Women 3*, lessons 12 and 14

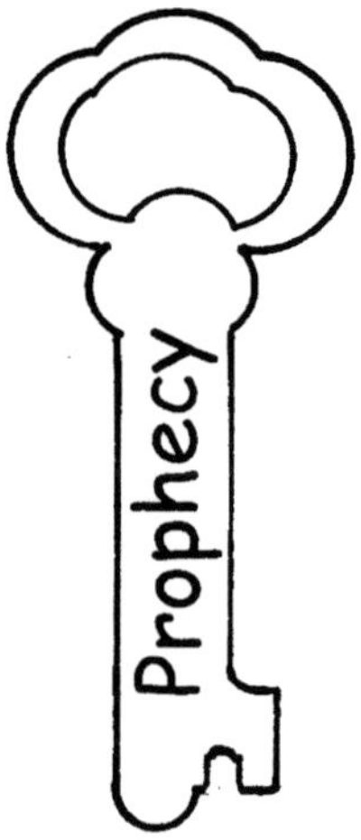
Prophecy

Authority

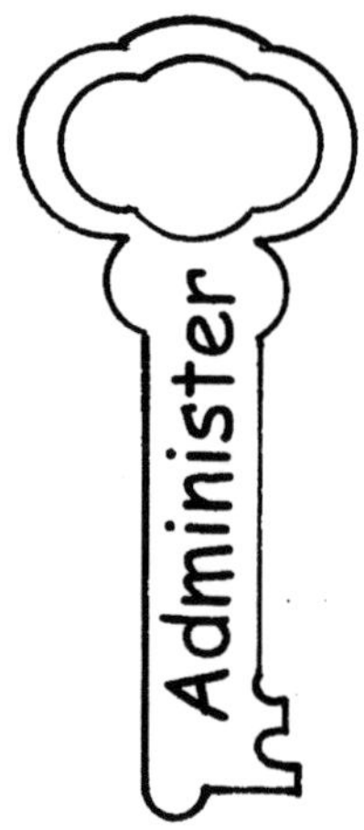
Administer

Called

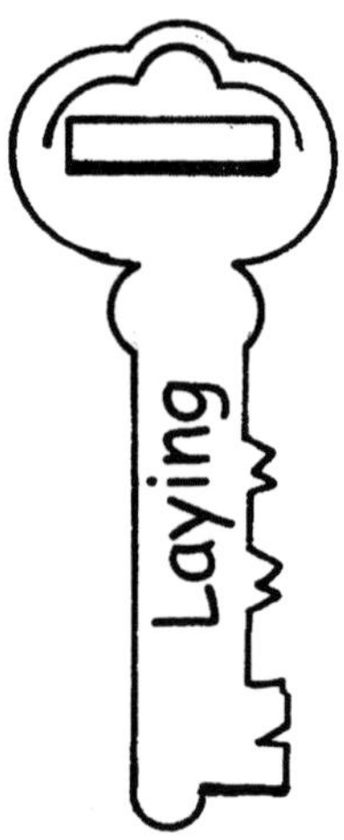
Laying

Ordinances

Six
The Sixth Article of Faith

Scripture: "And he gave some, apostles; and some prophets; and some pastors and teachers;"

—Ephesians 4:11-12

Song: "Tell Me the Stories of Jesus," *Children's Songbook*, pg. 57 or "The Sixth Article of Faith," *Children's Songbook*, pg. 125.

Treat: Pears

Lesson:

Materials Needed:

* Copy, color, cut and laminate the accompanying pictures of the heads of the church
* Chalkboard and chalk
* Tape

Write, "We believe in the same organization that existed in the Primitive Church" across the top of the chalkboard. Make a list down the middle of the chalkboard in order-apostles, prophets, pastors, teachers, and evangelists. In smaller letters to the bottom and side of the board, write "Anna Picks Pears to Eat."

Explain to the children that when Jesus was on the earth, He called people to help him lead and guide the church. Some of these men were called apostles; they were with Jesus most of the time when He was teaching. Have them name as many of the apostles as they can. Place the picture of the early apostles on the left side of the word "apostles" on the board. Ask the children if the church has apostles today, can they name any? Place the picture of the modern apostles on the right side of the word. Have the children recite The Sixth Article of Faith to this point.

Add the next word; ask the children to name some Old, New Testament and Book of Mormon prophets. Place the picture on the left. Now name some modern day prophets and place the picture on the right. Have the children recite the Sixth Article of Faith to this point.

Continue this process for the rest of the leaders named. Help them understand the correlation between the primitive church leaders and those we are familiar with today. Use available illustrations to help them visualize the stories and roles of different people.

A pastor is the same as a bishop. Paul and the leaders of the twelve tribes would be early bishops.

Teachers are missionaries and anyone past and present with a responsibility to share the gospel.

Evangelists are patriarchs. Examples of patriarchs in the early church would be anyone who gave a blessing of order and responsibility: such as a birthright.

When you have been through the entire Article of Faith and posted the pictures appropriately, show them that they can easily remember the order that they are mentioned in the article of faith by remembering the anagram you wrote on the board. "Anna Picks Pears To Eat" introduces the first letters of each leader in their proper order. Say the Article of Faith one more time, and then erase the list of leaders from the board. Have the children try repeating it appropriately. Try it again after removing the pictures.

Now use the pictures to play a memory game. Turn all the pictures face down in a random order. Have the children take turns trying to match the leaders from the two eras with their counter-parts. When a match is made have the child place the pictures back up on the board in their proper order once again.

With use of the game and the mnemonic device, the children should be almost ready to pass off this Article of Faith.

Activity:

Materials Needed:

* Several copies of the butterfly for each child
* Straws
* Washable tempera paint: 5 different colors
* Writing utensil
* Newspaper or other covering for the table

Encourage children to wear old clothes that won't be harmed by paint or stains.

Show the children the outline of the butterfly and ask them to tell you if they know what is special about a butterfly's wings. Butterfly wings have a special fuzzy coating on them that enables the butterfly to fly, and the patterns on them are mirror images from side to side.

Tell the children that the organization of the church is much the same as a butterfly's wings. We are lead by Jesus Christ; He gives us the power to return to him (to fly). He has given us a pattern for His church that gives us the leaders we need to help us. These are the same leaders that were in His church when He was on the earth.

Have the children repeat their names as listed in the article of faith once again, then show them the five colors of paint. There are five colors to represent each of the leaders they discussed from the Article of Faith. They will be coloring their butterfly wings to make mirror images just as you discussed that the leaders of Christ's church are the same in the past and the present.

Have the children carefully fold their butterfly exactly in half so that its wings match up evenly. Instruct them to write their names on the back of the picture.

Show the children how to use a straw and their finger to create a small suction to draw up paint into the end of the straw. Drop the different paints from the straws onto one side of butterfly wings. Remind the children to only put paint on one side of their wings. Allow them to drop paint onto their chosen wings until they feel satisfied with the results.

Then, show them how to gently fold the wings together and press down slightly to transfer some of their paint onto the other wings. Tell them not to rub—only press straight down or they will smear their pattern. When the wings have been touched together, open them back up to dry and observe the mirror patterns they have made.

Odds are they will want to repeat the process more than once.

Use this lesson to re-enforce:

* *Faith in God*, general requirements
* *Gospel Principles*, "The Articles of Faith" and chapters 16 and 17
* *Primary 1*, lesson 42
* *Primary 2*, lesson 42
* *Primary 3*, lesson 6
* *Primary 5*, lesson 11
* *Primary 7*, lesson 9

Apostle
Prophet
Apostle
Prophet

Pastor
Teacher
Pastor (Bishop)
Teacher (Missionary)

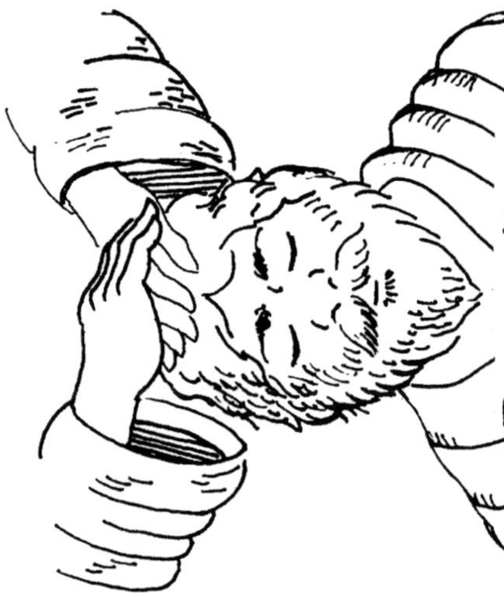

Evangelist

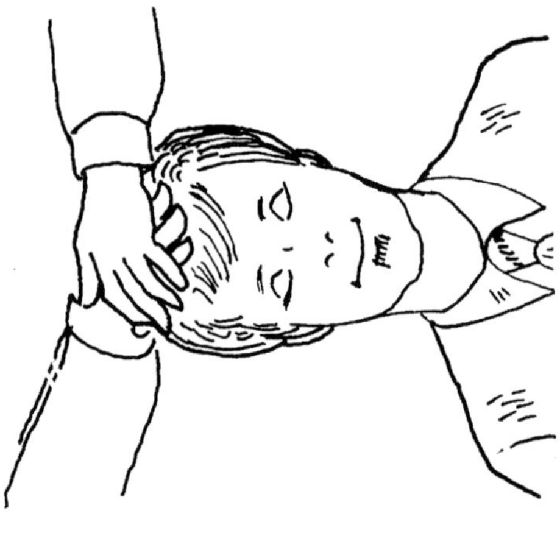

Evangelist (Patriarch)

Seven
The Seventh Article of Faith

Scripture: "But the manifestation of the Spirit is given to every man to profit withal"
—1 Corinthians 12:7-10

Song: "Every Star is Different," *Children's Songbook*, pg. 142 or "The Seventh Article of Faith," *Children's Songbook*, pg. 126.

Treat: Star shaped cookies or Jello® "jigglers"

Lesson:
Materials Needed:
* Wrapped gift box approximately shoe box size
* Chalkboard and chalk or dry erase board
* Scriptures for each child
* Scraps of paper with the gifts from the Article of Faith on them

Write the gifts of the spirit, listed in the Seventh Article of Faith, in a line down one side of the chalkboard. On the other side write the corresponding scripture story title in random order. Do not include the scripture reference on the board.

Show the children the wrapped gift. Ask them to tell you some reasons that we give or receive earthly gifts.

Then ask them to tell you about a favorite gift that they have received. Help the children understand that gifts are given to show friendship, love and appreciation. When we give a gift, we hope that we are giving that person something that will make them happy. How would it be if we always gave the same gift to everyone, no matter what the occasion or if the person would even like it? Would a power drill be an appropriate gift for a new baby?

Our Heavenly Father also gives us gifts and blessings. He blesses us with the things we need, or things that we can use to help others. Some of these gifts are called "gifts of the Spirit" and are mentioned in the Seventh Article of Faith. Read this Article of Faith to the children. Then read it again in sections so that the children can repeat it back to you.

Not everyone has all of these gifts, some may have gifts that aren't even mentioned in this statement, some may only have one and only for a short while when it is needed. The important thing to remember is that there are lots of gifts and occasions for giving and Heavenly Father is a generous and loving giver. If we stay true to the gospel, we'll always have just what we need to be happy and strengthen our own testimonies as well as the testimonies of others.

To understand what each of the gifts mentioned in the Article of Faith are, have the children look up the scripture stories and read them aloud. They should then identify the title of the story and try to match it with the gift it refers to. When they make a match, draw a line from the gift to the story.

* Gift of tongues—The Day of Pentecost (Acts 2:1-8)
* Prophecy—Samuel the Lamanite tells of the birth of Christ (Helaman 14:2-6)
* Revelation—Ammon before King Lamoni (Alma 18:15-17)
* Visions—The tree of life (1 Nephi 8:10-35)
* Healing—Naaman washes seven times (2 Kings 5:9-14)
* Interpretation of tongues—Christ appears to the Nephites (3 Nephi 11:3-7)

After all of the gifts have been identified from the scriptures, help the children discuss how that gift could be used in their own lives, or in the latter-days. Emphasize that these gifts are given through the Holy Ghost to those who are living worthily and are in need of them. They are special and precious and not to be taken lightly.

Have the children take turns drawing a gift from your scraps of paper. They are not to tell the other children what it is. Each of the other children gets to ask the child with the gift one "yes" or "no" question to see if they can guess what the gift is.

Activity:

Materials Needed:

* Wrapped gift box approximately shoe box size, used in above lesson
* Music player and appropriate music

Have the children form a circle, assign each the name of a gift from the Seventh Article of Faith, in order of mention (for simplicity use "tongues" for the gift of tongues, and "interpretation" for interpretation of tongues). If you have less than six children, go around the circle a second time till you run out of words.

Have them practice saying the words in order several times till they each have committed their assigned words to memory. Then give the first child the package. He or she is to say her word than pass it to the next child and so on. Go around and around trying to go faster with each pass till a mistake is made. If the box gets dropped or a child says the wrong word, or can't remember their word, play must begin again from the beginning.

Next, turn on the music and have the children silently pass the gift as one would to play "hot potato." Stop the music at intervals, the child caught holding the gift must name all the gifts in order. If they can not, they are out of the game for one round.

By the end of this activity most of the children should be ready to begin passing off the memorization of this article of faith.

Use this lesson to re-enforce:

* *Faith in God*, general requirements
* *Gospel Principles*, "The Articles of Faith"
* *Family Home Evening Resource Book*, lesson ideas "talents and gifts"

* *Primary 3*, lesson 24
* *Primary 5*, lesson 19
* *Primary 7*, lesson 45
* *New Testament Gospel Doctrine Manual*, lesson 46
* *Aaronic Priesthood 2*, lesson 32

Eight
The Eighth Article of Faith

Scripture: "And again, the elders, priests and teachers of this church shall teach the principles of my gospel, which are in the Bible and the Book of Mormon, in the which is the fullness of the gospel."

—D&C 42:12

Song: "Search, Ponder, and Pray," *Children's Songbook*, pg. 109 or "The Eighth Article of Faith," *Children's Songbook*, pg. 127.

Treat: "Papyrus scrolls"—fruit leather roll-ups

Lesson:
Materials Needed:
* A copy of the coded message for each child
* Writing utensils for each child

Ask the children how many different ways we have today to make a record of something we want to remember.

Now ask them to name some of the different languages people speak around the world.

Ask them to share their ideas on how Heavenly Father would be able to help all the different people in the world know his gospel.

Remind the children that the world has not always had the technology and abilities that we do today for making and keeping records. Many years ago, not everyone could even write or read: they simply had to remember things that were told to them. When they told someone else they sometimes didn't remember things the same way they were first told.

At this point you can play the "telephone" game with the children to illustrate how things could change.

People, who could read and write, tried to keep things written down, but their papers didn't always last very long. Sometimes other people would try to carefully copy what others had written; it didn't always get copied right. Other times, they didn't speak the same language and had to translate what was written, or they wanted to make it easier for people to understand so they changed some of the words.

Have the children translate your coded words, then make a coded word of their own and trade papers with another child. That child will try to translate what the new word is and so on. Emphasize to the children how easily mistakes can be made while doing this.

Tell the children that those who tried to preserve Heavenly Father's teachings in the Bible sometimes made these types of mistakes. We have been directed to use the King James Version of the Bible because it has the fewest mistakes.

Ask the children what is different about The Book of Mormon. When Joseph Smith received the brass plates from Moroni, he was also given a gift to help him translate the words written there exactly as Heavenly Father wanted us to have them. This gift was the Urim and Thummim. It still wasn't easy and took a long time, but we now know exactly what the prophets in the Americas really wanted us to hear about Jesus and His gospel.

When we study both the Bible and the Book of Mormon we can know a lot of Jesus' teachings.

Bear your testimony of the importance of the scriptures and the special spirit studying them can bring into your life. Also express gratitude for living prophets and Joseph Smith's work in bring words of earlier prophets to us.

Review the Eighth Article of Faith with the children by breaking it into two parts. Discuss what you learned about the Bible and then about the Book of Mormon and have the children repeat each part of the statement with you several times.

Activity:

Materials Needed:

* 1 large serving tray
* A variety of items from your home (such as a *Book of Mormon*, a pen, a small picture, a kitchen utensil, stapler, small piece of candy, etc.) try to have at least 20 items of varying sizes and uses.
* Paper for each child
* Writing utensils for each child
* A cloth to cover the tray or a way to block it from the children's sight
* Timer or watch
* Chalkboard and chalk or other way to display final list

Show the children your tray of items, and tell them they will have one minute to try and remember everything they see so that they can write it down when the tray has been removed from their sight. Allow them to look and make comments for one minute then cover the tray.

Choose one child at random to be your special helper. Allow him to sit with the tray, away from the other children's view, and make a master list of its contents while the other children try to make their lists from memory.

After everyone has finished, allow the children to share their answers. Write a collective answer list on the board. Then, allow the child with the master list to share his answers. Ask the children to share their feelings as to why his answers were all correct and theirs were not. Prompt them to notice that everyone remembered the same things or had a complete list and remind them that this is what has happened to the bible over time. Did anyone list an item that was never on the tray? Discuss how this could have happened. Remind them that the Book of Mormon is different because Joseph Smith had the original in front of him as he wrote down what the Lord wanted us to know.

For additional variation show the tray again. Then hide it while you remove one item from it. Show it to the children again and have them guess what is missing without looking at their previous answer sheets. Repeat this several times. This helps to show them that even though some things may have been left out of the Bible, or changed along the way, it is still Heavenly Fathers words for us. We can be helped to know what has been changed or missing through studying all of our scriptures together. Joseph Smith also spent some time going back through the Bible and listening for Heavenly Father's revelations to fix some of the mistakes. The things he fixed are found in the footnotes of our bibles and in *Joseph Smith–Matthew* in *The Pearl of Great Price.*

Use this lesson to re-enforce:

* *Faith in God*, general requirements
* Cub Scouts, Wolf Electives 1a and 22
* *Gospel Principles*, "The Articles of Faith"
* *Family Home Evening Resource Book*, lesson 4
* *Primary 1*, lesson 41
* *Primary 3*, lessons 15 and 17
* *Primary 4*, lesson 1
* *Primary 5*, lessons 10 and 20
* *Primary 7*, lesson 1
* *Doctrine and Covenants and Church History Gospel Doctrine Manual*, lesson 13

Secret Code Key

A	B	C	D	E	F	G
チ	ツ	テ	ト	ナ	ニ	ヌ
H	I	J	K	L	M	N
ネ	ノ	ハ	ヒ	フ	ヘ	ホ
O	P	Q	R	S	T	U
マ	ミ	ム	メ	モ	ヤ	ユ
	V	W	X	Y	Z	
	ヨ	ラ	リ	ル	レ	

Decode the Following Secret Message

ヤ メ チ ホ モ フ チ ヤ ナ

_ _ _ _ _ _ _ _ _

ノ ヤ

_ _

テ マ メ メ ナ テ ヤ フ ル

_ _ _ _ _ _ _ _ _

Nine
The Ninth Article of Faith

Scripture: "God shall give unto you knowledge by his Holy Spirit, yea, by the unspeakable gift of the Holy Ghost, that has not been revealed since the world was until now; Which our forefather have awaited with anxious expectation to be revealed in the last times, which their minds were pointed to by the angels, as held in reserve for the fullness of their glory."

—D&C 121:26-27

Song: "Tell me, Dear Lord," *Children's Songbook*, pg. 176 or "The Ninth Article of Faith," *Children's Songbook*, pg. 128.

Treat: Triple-layered dessert or Jello®

Lesson:
Materials Needed:
* 500 piece puzzle with accompanying illustration (unless you have a very small group larger puzzles are best)

Before the lesson: put together approximately 50 pieces of the puzzle. Try to choose a portion that doesn't make it obvious what the entire puzzle depicts.

Show the children the pieces of the puzzle that you put together before the activity, but keep the illustration hidden from view. Ask them to guess what they think the whole puzzle would look like. Allow them each to voice their thoughts. Why it is difficult to tell what the picture could be? (All of the pieces aren't there.)

Give the children an additional random handful of pieces and ask them to try placing them and continue to guess what the puzzle is. Refuse any requests to see the illustration; instead hand them a few more pieces.

Ask a child to read The Ninth Article of Faith. Let them review what they think it means with you. Show them that revelation from Heavenly Father is like the puzzle in front of them. There are things that Heavenly Father has told us before, some times long before, that we can put together and use to make our lives better. Suggest some of these things and let them think of others. Suggestions could include the Word of Wisdom, Tithing, The Ten Commandments, and Lehi being told to leave Jerusalem. This is what it means when we say that we believe "all that god has revealed."

Ask the children if just these things make a complete puzzle or picture (no). Even though we have received many useful revelations, there are still things we need to know now that will help us live better lives. That is why we have a living prophet today. He shares more pieces of the puzzle with us every day. Help them think of things the prophets have said recently; such as, the building of smaller temples or the perpetual education fund, remind them that revelations are not always big but are always important. The decisions made every day by the prophet as to how the church's funds should be used and where missionaries should be sent are just as important to the gospel as the big things. These are the types of things we are talking about when we say we believe "all that He does now reveal." Remind the children that they are also entitled to their own personal revelations that will help them even further.

Tell the children that the Lord has promised us that we will always have a prophet to tell us what we need to know. We can trust that the Lord will make further revelations, in the same manner that He always has, to help us grow closer to Him. "We believe that he will yet reveal many great and important things pertaining to the kingdom of God."

Show the children the illustration for the puzzle, remind them that Heavenly Father always knows what the whole picture should and will look like, but we may not. We have the Holy Spirit to let us know that revelations are true and to give us encouragement in following his plan or picture for us. When we ask Him, we may not get to see that picture, but He will always provide more help to get us closer to Him.

Activity:

Materials Needed:

* Partially finished puzzle from the lesson

Let the children try to finish the puzzle you brought while they practice memorizing and passing off this Article of Faith.

To help the children with the memorization process, remind them that this Article of Faith has three parts. It talks about revelation past, present and future. See if they can work on memorizing it in those three sections and then put them together. It might also help to have them stand up and move their bodies to different positions for each section. For instance they might move as if they were on different sections of a time line.

Use this lesson to re-enforce:

* *Faith in God*, general requirements
* *Gospel Principles*, "The Articles of Faith"
* *Family Home Evening Resource Book*, lesson 7
* *Primary 2*, lesson 13
* *Primary 3*, lesson 12
* *Primary 4*, lesson 2
* *Primary 5*, lesson 36
* *New Testament Gospel Doctrine Manual*, lesson 40

Ten
The Tenth Article of Faith

Scripture: "Nevertheless, when that day cometh, saith the prophet, that they no more turn aside their hearts against the Holy One of Israel, then will he remember the covenants which he made to their fathers. Yea, then will he remember the isles of the sea; yea, and all the people who are of the house of Israel, will I gather in, saith the Lord, according to the words of the prophet Zenos, from the four quarters of the earth. Yea, and all the earth shall see the salvation of the Lord, saith the prophet; every nation, kindred, tongue and people shall be blessed."

—1 Nephi 19:15-17

Song: "Children All Over the World," *Children's Songbook*, pg. 16 or "The Tenth Article of Faith," *Children's Songbook*, pg. 128.

Treat: Marshmallow Sheep—roll large marshmallows in melted white chocolate than in shredded coconut. Attach small marshmallows for head and legs with toothpicks or more dabs of melted chocolate.

Lesson:

Materials Needed:

* Chalkboard and chalk, or dry-erase board and marker
* Appropriate eraser

Write the words to the Article of Faith on the board. Underline the following terms: literal, gathering, Israel, restoration, Ten Tribes, Zion, reign, renewed, paradisiacal glory.

Read through the Tenth Article of Faith with the children. Tell them that you have identified some words that they will be learning about. As each word is discussed it will be erased from the Article of Faith. When each word has been defined and reviewed, erase the word then have the children read the Article of Faith again reinserting the missing words from memory.

This article of faith refers to a story from the Old Testament, The Lord blessed a man named Jacob with a new name that meant "prince of God," that name was Israel. He was also blessed with twelve sons. As they grew and had families of their own, they became known as the twelve tribes of Israel.

As time went on, ten of the tribes became lost, due to wars and other hardships. We don't have any records that tell us where they are or what happened to them. Remind them that even though we may not know where they are, they are not lost to Heavenly Father. We have been promised that before Christ comes again, everyone will be able

to hear about the gospel and those who accept it will be gathered together into one fold, or family, again.
* Literal—exact, precise, not figurative or made-up.
* Gathering—to bring together.
* Israel—the man Jacob and his descendants, those who believe in Christ.
* Restoration—returning something to its original condition, to make whole.
* Ten Tribes—those groups of people whose records and whereabouts have been lost to us.
* Zion, the New Jerusalem—a place for the "pure in heart" or true followers of Christ.
* Reign—to rule or preside over
* Renewed—to become like new again, perfected
* Paradisiacal glory—a condition of happiness and peace, glorified and perfect.

Review this article of faith several more times until the children are comfortable with all the words and can remember those that have been "lost." See if you can erase even more words until the whole statement has been memorized!

Activity:

Materials Needed:
* Large stack of chairs, teaching tables, other items that can be used as obstacles
* Enough blindfolds for all the children
* Large room or area to move around in

Have the children place the chairs and obstacles all over the room until it forms a maze-type coarse. Explain to the children that Christ is sometimes called the "good shepherd." He leads and guides and will gather all of the earth's children to Him when he comes again. No one is lost to Him.

Choose one child to be the shepherd. He or she will stand in the middle of the maze (you might put him on a chair to give him a better view of the whole room).

Blindfold all the children, other than the shepherd, and then lead them each to different corners of the room.

This game is played out similarly to "Mother May I." The blindfolded children must stand where they are and wait for the shepherd to call to them. He or she will call the child by their name and say "(child's name) you may take ____ steps forward." The child must then ask "Shepherd May I?" The shepherd answers in the affirmative and the child proceeds to move as the shepherd told him to.

The shepherd must call on every child in turn and give them directions that will safely lead each child to him or her. He may vary the number or style of steps as needed (i.e. small, giant, left, right, twirling, etc.), but he may not purposely lead them astray.

The lost sheep may only follow through with the commands of the shepherd if they first remember to ask permission. If they do not say "Shepherd may I?" then their turn is forfeited.

The game ends when all the sheep have been safely brought to the shepherd.

Use this lesson to re-enforce:
* *Faith in God*, general requirements

* *Gospel Principles*, “The Articles of Faith”
* *Primary 5*, lesson 29
* *Primary 6*, lesson 19
* *Primary 7*, lesson 46
* *Doctrine and Covenants and Church History Gospel Doctrine Manual*, lessons 12 and 21

Eleven
The Eleventh Article of Faith

Scripture: "We believe that religion is instituted of God; and that men are amenable to him, and to him only, for the exercise of it, unless their religious opinions prompt them to infringe upon the rights and liberties of others; but we do not believe that human law has a right to interfere in prescribing rules of worship to bind the consciences of men, nor dictate forms for public or private devotion; that the civil magistrate should restrain crime, but never control conscience; should punish guilt, but never suppress the freedom of the soul."

—D&C 134:4

Song: "We Are Different," *Children's Songbook*, pg. 263 or "The Eleventh Article of Faith," *Children's Songbook*, pg. 130.

Treat: Taster's table of foods from different cultures

Lesson:

Materials Needed:

* World map

Prior to this activity night, assign each child one of the six major world religions to research. They will provide the lessons on this evening by presenting some of the things they learned about their assigned topic. Help them locate the place of origin and tell what the basic beliefs are. Encourage them to dress-up, provide an appropriate ethnic snack, and activity as available and appropriate. Each presentation only needs to be 10-15 minutes long.

The world's six major religions are: Judaism, Christianity, Islam, Hinduism, Buddhism, and Confucianism/Taoism. If you have more than six children team them up to work together.

Good reference books that put information about religions in child friendly format are:

* *Eyewitness Books: Religion* by Myrtle Langley
* *One World, Many Religions: The Way We Worship* by Mary Pope Osborn.

Activity:

Materials Needed:

* Large poster board with The Eleventh Article of Faith on it

* Index cards with the words privilege, worshiping, dictates, conscience, how, where and what
* Blindfold
* Tape

Have the children take turns drawing an index card, then blind fold them and play "pin the word to the Article of Faith" see how close they can come to placing the word in its appropriate spot in the statement. This is also a good time to review the meaning of the more difficult words in this Article of Faith. These activities will increase their familiarity with the statement and its order to aid in memorization.

Use this lesson to re-enforce:

* *Faith in God*, general requirements
* *Gospel Principles*, "The Articles of Faith"
* *Family Home Evening Resource Book*, lesson 24
* *Primary 5*, lesson 36

Twelve
The Twelfth Article of Faith

Scripture: "We believe that governments were instituted of God for the benefit of man; and that he hold men accountable for their acts in relation to them, both in making laws and administering them, for the good and safety of society."

—D&C 134:1

Song: "My Country," *Children's Songbook*, pg. 224 or "The Twelfth Article of Faith," *Children's Songbook*, pg. 131.

Treat: Frost a rectangular cake with white icing, use red and blue M&M's® to make an American flag design

Lesson:
Materials Needed:
* Copy of the *Webelos Scout Book* pg. 159-175
* *Children's Songbook* pg. 131, accompaniment if available

In a prior activity night let the children choose one of the following subjects to research and give a 5-10 minute presentation on at this meeting. Children may double up if you have more than the below listed topics or add more topics as needed.

* The flag
* The Constitution
* The Statue of Liberty
* The Star-spangled Banner
* The Pledge of Allegiance
* Elections and Presidencies
* The Fourth of July

Review the citizenship portion of the *Webelos Scout Book* prior to this meeting.

Share with the children the privilege that living in the United States is. Help them understand that by showing proper patriotism, we are showing our gratitude for the blessing that it is to live here.

Discuss ways they can show proper respect and thankfulness for the blessing of living in this country.

Use the song from the *Children's Songbook* to help the children learn this Article of Faith.

Activity:

Materials Needed:

* Large sheet or flag if available
* Copies of Hymns #338-340
* Hymn accompaniment if available
* Copy of the *Webelos Scout Book* pgs. 159-175

Show the children how to fold a flag properly, according to the instructions from your scouting manual.

Help them sing the songs of our nation.

Use this lesson to re-enforce:

* *Faith in God*, general requirements, and serving others
* Cub Scouts, Wolf Achievement 2, Bear Achievement 3, Webelos "Citizen" badge
* *Gospel Principles*, "The Articles of Faith"
* *Family Home Evening Resource Book*, lesson ideas "citizenship"
* Primary 5, lesson 36
* *Doctrine and Covenants and Church History Gospel Doctrine Manual*, lesson 44

Thirteen
The Thirteenth Article of Faith

Scripture: "Finally, brethren, whatsoever things are true, whatsoever things are honest, whatsoever things are just, whatsoever things are pure, whatsoever things are lovely, whatsoever things are of good report; if there be any virtue, and if there be any praise, think on these things."

—Philippians 4:8

Song: "Beauty Everywhere," *Children's Songbook*, pg. 232 or "The Thirteenth Article of Faith," *Children's Songbook*, pg. 132.

Treat: Nestle® Chocolate Treasures

Lesson:
Materials Needed:
* Printed copy of The Thirteenth Article of Faith for each child
* Highlighter or other marking utensil
* Copies of the word treasure chests, enough for each child, colored and cut out
* Copies of the section "Dress and Appearance" from the church produced pamphlet *For the Strength of Youth*, 2001

Hide the treasure chests around the area of your lesson. Give each child a copy of The Thirteenth Article of Faith with the words from the treasure chests highlighted. Have each child find a complete set of treasure chests. If one child finds a duplicate treasure he must find someone else to trade it with or just give it to someone who needs it.

Place a set of treasure chests on the board in their correct order and let the children give their ideas as to what each one means, and why Joseph Smith would have included them in this statement.

Help them discuss ways that they can seek these types of things every day in the choices they make. Explain that we are children of Heavenly Father who sees great goodness and beauty in each of us. We can honor him by keeping our bodies and the things around us worthy of Him. Read the Dress and Appearance section of *For the Strength of Youth* with them. Several other sections may also be covered at this time if you feel it is appropriate for your group.

Write in a few hint words around each of the treasure chests. Go through the full Article of Faith several times trying to use only the prompts from the board.

Show them the appropriate sign language gestures that correspond to the words from the statement. Review the statement a few more times and then remove the treasure chests, as the children master each corresponding gesture. Now have the children try reciting the whole statement again. To help the children, when they come to a word missing from the statement, sign it for them but do not say it. Let them begin to associate the words and signs. This will help with the memorization process and familiarity of the terms.

If you are working with a group of Webelos, this is also an excellent time to introduce the Boy Scout Law.

Activity:

Materials Needed:

* Printed copy of the word search "We Seek After These Things"

Allow the children to work on their word search and continue to become familiar with the terms used in this Article of Faith.

Use this lesson to re-enforce:

* *Faith in God*, general requirements, preparing for Young Women and preparing for the Priesthood
* *Gospel Principles*, "The Articles of Faith" and chapter 31
* *My Gospel Standards*
* *Family Home Evening Resource Book*, lesson idea "media"
* *Primary 1*, lesson 37
* *Primary 2*, lesson 34
* *Primary 4*, lesson 38
* *Primary 5*, lesson 36
* *Young Women 2*, lessons 36, 45 and 47
* *For the Strength of Youth*, "Dress and Appearance"

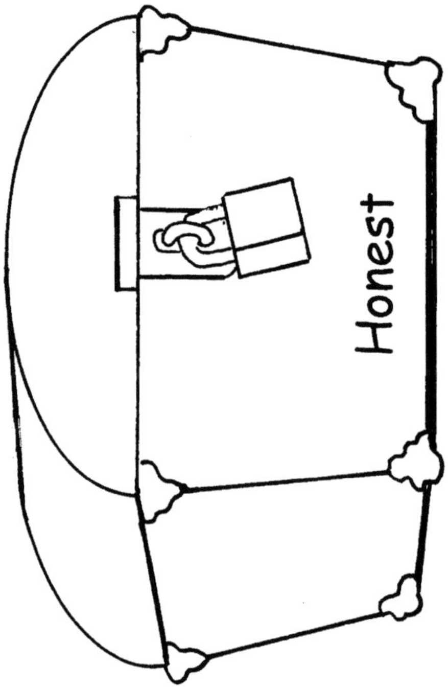
Honest

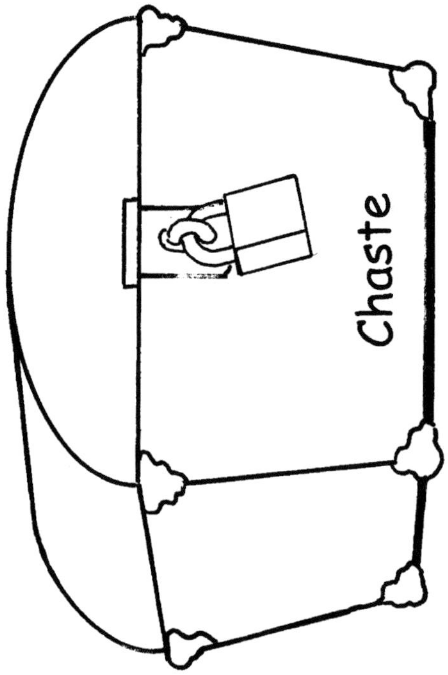
Chaste

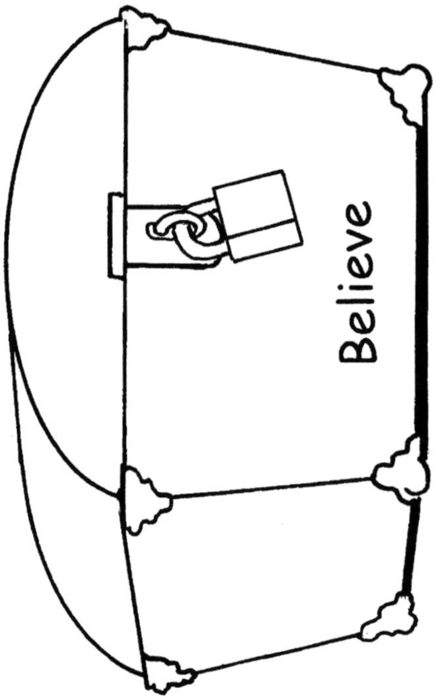
Believe

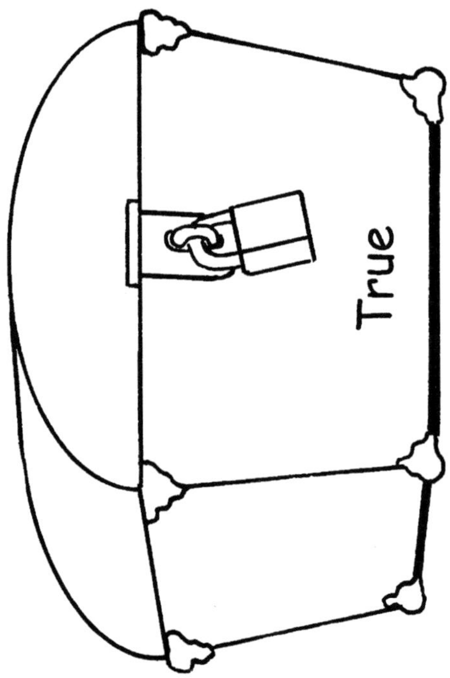
True

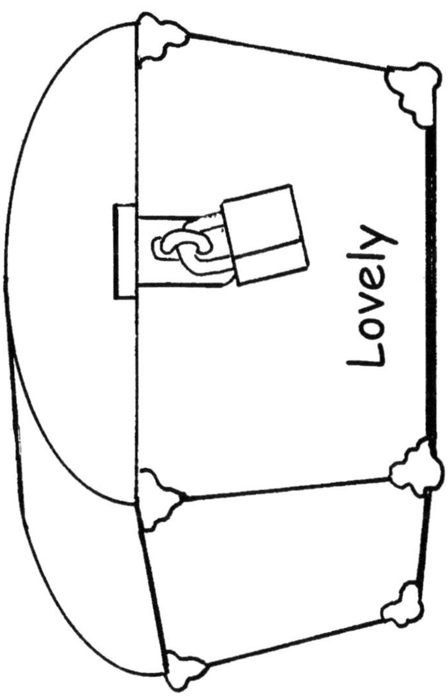
Lovely

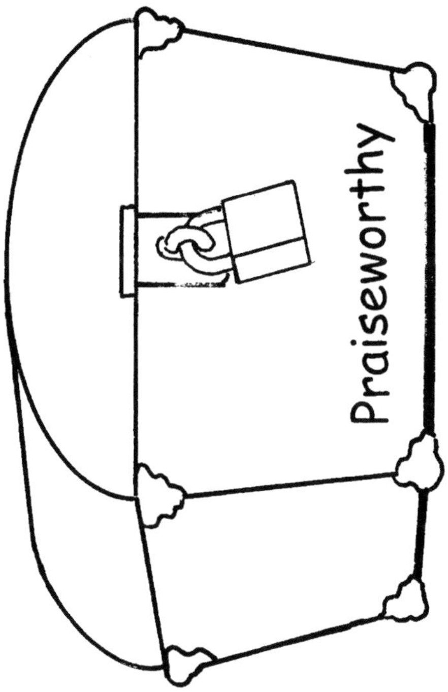
Praiseworthy

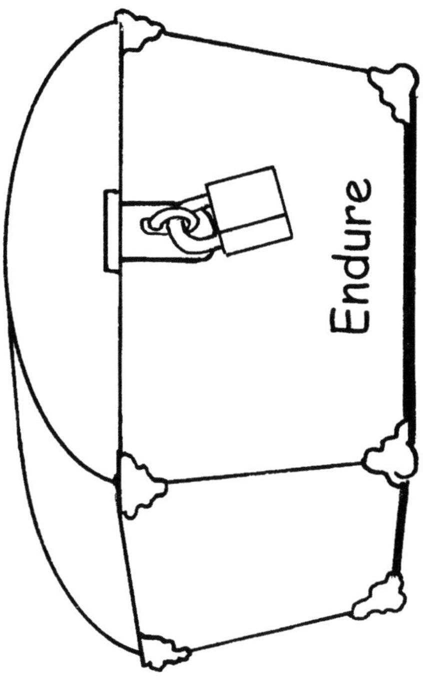
Endure

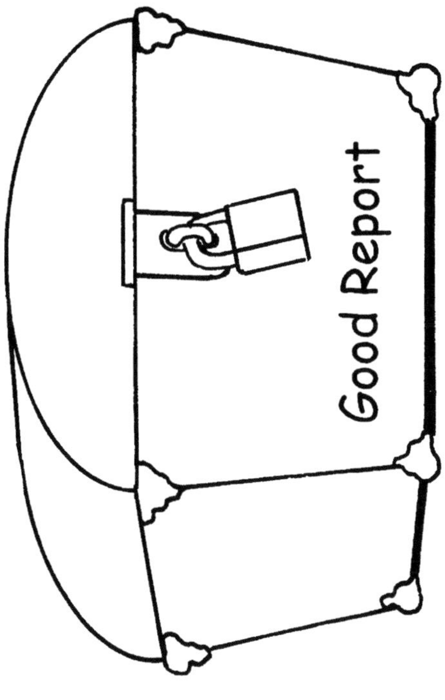
Good Report

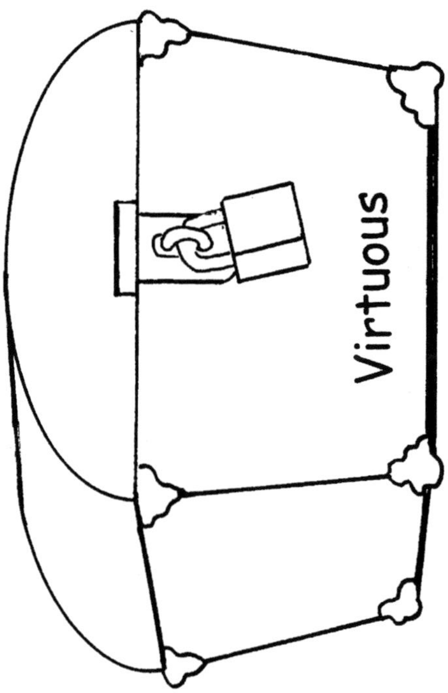
Virtuous

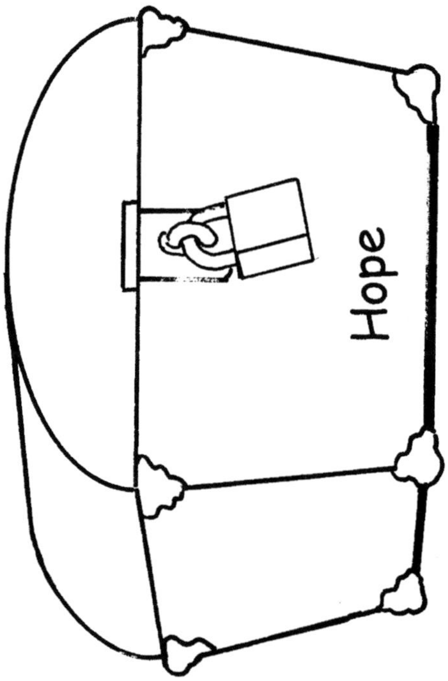
Hope

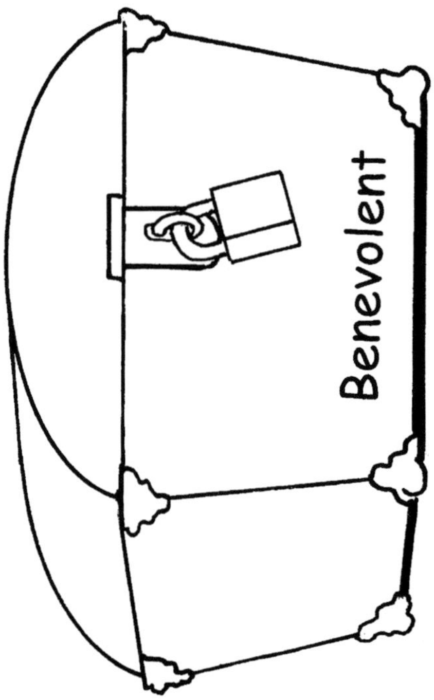
Benevolent

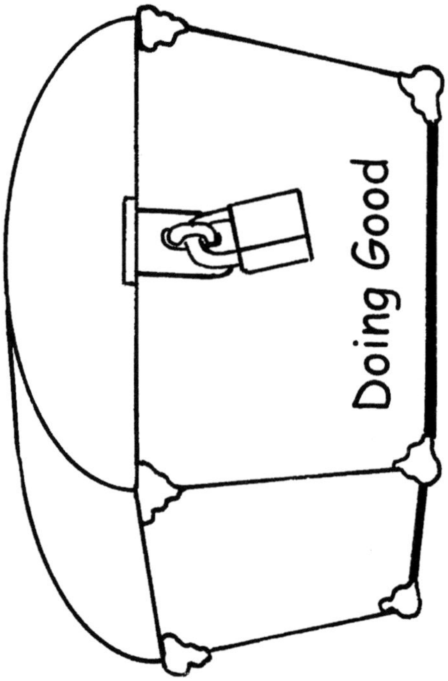
Doing Good

Believe

Good

Seek

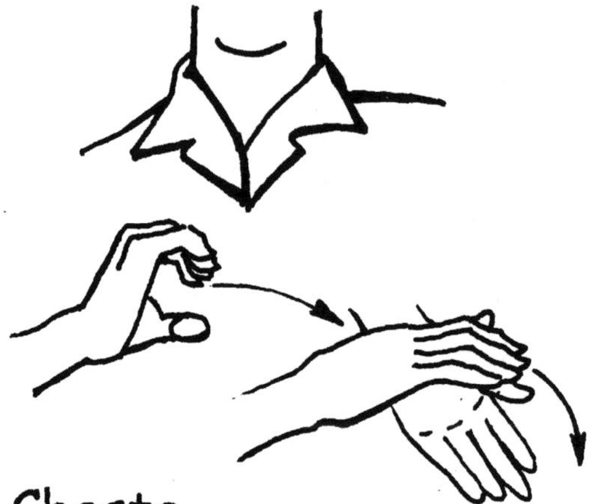

Chaste
Virtuous

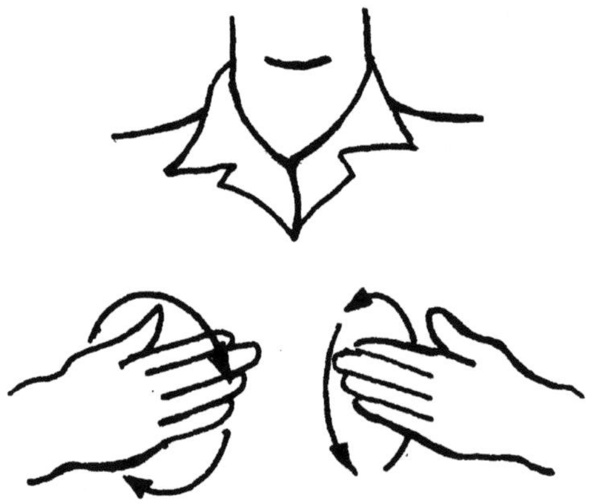

Benevolent

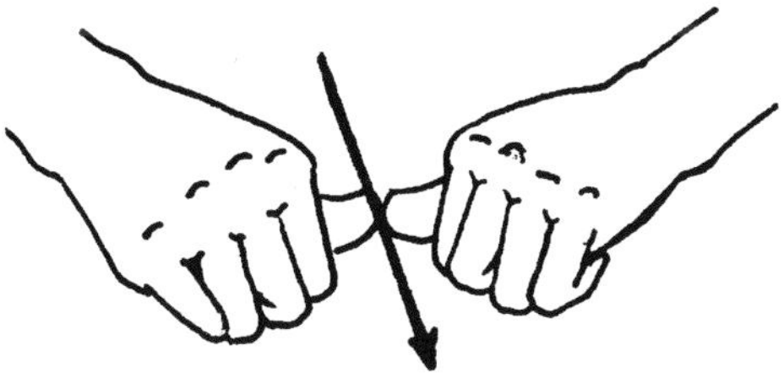

Endure

Honest

True

Lovely

Praiseworthy
(Worthy)

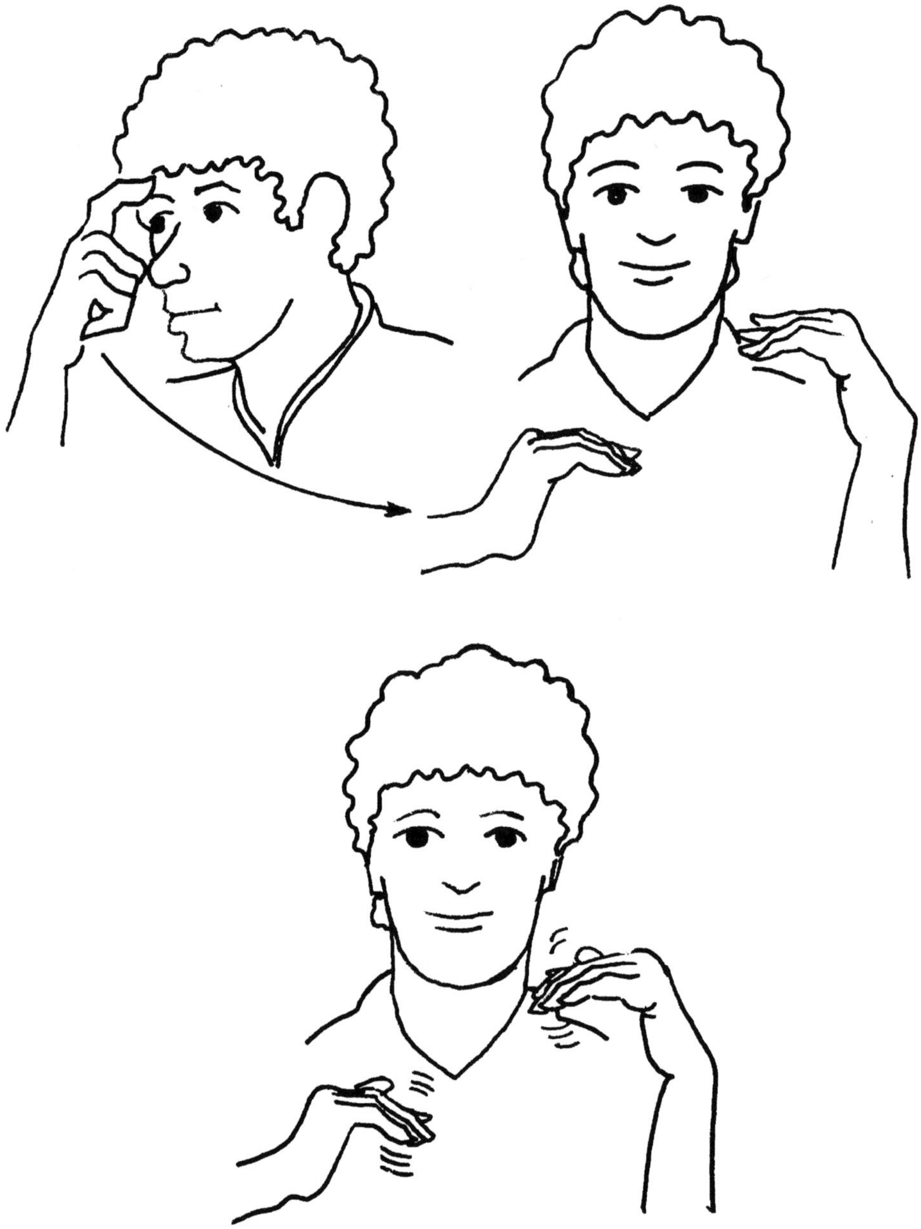

Hope

WE SEEK AFTER THESE THINGS

A	B	C	D	E	C	H	E	E	R	F	U	L	O	P	E	D	Y	G	S	P
B	A	R	T	I	C	L	E	G	O	O	I	A	W	I	G	R	O	Y	A	O
C	M	D	I	S	G	O	B	P	Y	Q	S	F	C	J	R	O	R	M	S	B
D	A	K	R	M	E	V	M	D	A	H	I	Y	U	A	D	B	V	C	R	E
C	Z	O	W	O	Y	E	V	A	L	A	Y	O	L	U	W	E	R	A	Z	L
O	S	W	H	D	T	L	N	O	Z	T	S	R	I	P	E	D	V	E	I	I
U	F	R	I	E	N	Y	K	B	F	D	E	N	V	P	O	I	Y	F	H	E
R	D	N	U	S	A	C	H	I	A	I	E	U	I	T	T	E	A	Q	B	V
T	R	U	S	T	W	O	R	T	H	Y	A	U	R	T	A	N	J	W	A	E
E	T	E	C	O	G	H	T	Y	R	O	S	O	T	T	M	T	V	E	R	S
O	T	Y	V	P	T	O	N	R	I	O	P	K	U	P	O	N	T	R	D	M
U	H	B	V	E	H	T	E	M	F	E	W	E	O	B	T	E	K	T	K	O
S	I	I	F	P	R	S	L	J	R	A	I	E	U	E	C	R	A	Y	P	S
O	R	J	B	O	B	G	O	D	B	E	B	S	S	X	K	E	Y	I	G	C
E	T	S	A	H	C	N	V	W	H	W	B	U	P	I	T	V	N	M	A	L
V	E	P	M	R	O	T	E	U	F	T	X	M	N	H	A	E	U	C	U	E
A	E	B	U	C	O	N	N	N	S	T	G	D	U	F	O	R	W	F	Y	A
R	N	Z	W	F	R	I	E	N	D	L	Y	V	B	C	P	J	P	R	I	N
B	A	K	D	I	G	R	B	S	B	U	W	M	R	G	U	L	H	D	K	X
S	N	D	I	Y	N	A	P	A	T	A	R	I	Y	N	E	C	A	Z	I	Y
Q	S	A	D	M	O	N	I	T	I	O	N	E	O	H	U	V	W	X	Y	Z

Admonition
Believe
Benevolent
Brave
Chaste
Cheerful
Clean
Courteous
Endure

Friendly
Good
Helpful
Honest
Hope
Kind
Lovely
Loyal
Modest

Obedient
Praiseworthy
Report
Reverent
Seek
Thrifty
True
Trustworthy
Virtuous

WE SEEK AFTER THESE THINGS

A	B	C	D	E	C	H	E	E	R	F	U	L	O	P	E	D	Y	G	S	P
B	A	R	T	I	C	L	E	G	O	O	I	A	W	I	G	R	O	Y	A	O
C	M	D	I	S	G	O	B	P	Y	Q	S	F	C	J	R	O	R	M	S	B
D	A	K	R	M	E	V	M	D	A	H	I	Y	U	A	D	B	V	C	R	E
C	Z	O	W	O	Y	E	V	A	L	A	Y	O	L	U	W	E	R	A	Z	L
O	S	W	H	D	T	L	N	O	Z	T	S	R	I	P	E	D	V	E	I	I
U	F	R	I	E	N	Y	K	B	F	D	E	N	Y	P	O	I	Y	F	H	E
R	D	N	U	S	A	C	H	I	A	I	E	U	I	T	T	E	A	Q	B	V
T	R	U	S	T	W	O	R	T	H	Y	A	U	R	T	A	N	J	W	A	E
E	T	E	C	O	G	H	T	Y	R	O	S	O	T	T	M	T	V	E	R	S
O	T	Y	V	P	T	O	N	R	I	O	P	K	U	P	O	N	T	R	D	M
U	H	B	V	E	H	T	E	M	F	E	W	E	O	B	T	E	K	T	K	O
S	I	I	F	P	R	S	L	J	R	A	I	E	U	E	C	R	A	Y	P	S
O	R	J	B	O	B	G	O	D	B	E	B	S	S	X	K	E	Y	I	G	C
E	T	S	A	H	C	N	V	W	H	W	B	U	P	E	T	V	N	M	A	L
V	E	P	M	R	O	T	E	U	F	T	X	M	N	H	A	E	U	C	U	E
A	E	B	U	C	O	N	N	N	S	T	G	D	U	F	O	R	W	F	Y	A
R	N	Z	W	F	R	I	E	N	D	L	Y	V	B	C	P	J	P	R	I	N
B	A	K	D	I	G	R	B	S	B	U	W	M	R	G	U	L	H	D	K	X
S	N	D	I	Y	N	A	P	A	T	A	R	I	Y	N	E	C	A	Z	I	Y
Q	S	A	D	M	O	N	I	T	I	O	N	E	O	H	U	V	W	X	Y	Z

Admonition	Friendly	Obedient
Believe	Good	Praiseworthy
Benevolent	Helpful	Report
Brave	Honest	Reverent
Chaste	Hope	Seek
Cheerful	Kind	Thrifty
Clean	Lovely	True
Courteous	Loyal	Trustworthy
Endure	Modest	Virtuous

Fourteen
Book of Mormon Stories

Scripture: "And upon these I write the things of my soul, and many of the scriptures which are engraven upon the plates of brass. For my soul delighteth in the scriptures, and my heart pondereth them, and writeth them for the learning and the profit of my children."

—2 Nephi 4:15

Song: "Book of Mormon Stories," *Children's Songbook*, pg. 118.

Treat: Ammon's Arm Soup

Lesson:
Materials needed:
* 1# of ground beef
* 1 small onion finely chopped
* 1 small green pepper finely chopped
* 6 cups of hot water
* 2 (15 oz) cans beef broth
* 2 carrots peeled and diced
* 3-4 potatoes peeled and diced
* 6 oz box of elbow macaroni
* 1 (14 oz) can Italian seasoned diced tomatoes
* 1 (14 oz) can tomato sauce
* 1 can of whole kernel corn, drained
* Salt and pepper to season
* Lrg. cooking pot with lid
* Lrg. wooden spoon
* Ladle
* Bowls
* Spoons
* Napkins
* A copy of the story-recipe for "Ammon's Arm Soup"
* Serves: Twelve

Note: please check your building's kitchen policies and comply with them. This may need to be an activity done within a home.

Be familiar with the story of Ammon and the king's sheep found in Alma 17:18—18:10. Read over this story-recipe several times and highlight the cooking process so that nothing gets overlooked.

Allow children to choose a grab bag at waiting points in the story of Ammon and the King's Sheep. They should guess what story is in the bag by the Gospel Art Picture and use it as a guide for telling the story if they aren't familiar with it. Let them act out the stories with the props that they will find in each bag.

Tell the following story, as you help the children complete this recipe.

"Ammon's Arm Soup"

"When Ammon went before King Lamoni he asked to be the King's servant and was assigned to help watch over his flocks. Can you pretend that this hamburger is the King's sheep and 'herd' (stir) them while the meat cooks?" Place the meat in cooking pot over medium heat, allow meat to partially cook.

"Let's add some fleece (onion) and some grass (green peppers) for them to eat."

Stir these three ingredients together until meat is completely browned.

"Ammon and the King's other servants took the sheep to get some water at the river" Add the hot water.

"But some robber's came across the river to scare the sheep away so they could steal them, I'm sure that made the water muddy" Add the broth.

"The robbers scared the sheep and made them run away from the servants. The servants were scared and didn't know what to do." Tell the children they will have to wait a bit for the servants to decide what to do. You will tell them the next part of the story after the soup begins to boil.

While waiting for the soup to boil have the children choose the first grab bag.

"Ammon helped the other servants gather up the sheep and showed the servants how to protect them if the robbers came again. When the sheep had all been gathered up, the robbers came back and tried to scare the sheep away again! But this time Ammon was ready. He began throwing stones at the robbers and everyone he hit fell down. Let's put some stones in with our water and sheep and see if we can scare the robbers away." Add the carrots and potatoes.

Allow vegetables to begin cooking about 7 minutes. And use a second grab bag.

"Throwing stones and fighting back really scared some of the robbers, but it made others really mad. They began trying to hurt Ammon with their clubs." Add macaroni clubs to the soup, and tomato products. Heavenly Father wouldn't let them hurt Ammon, so whenever one of the robbers raised his arm to hit Ammon, Ammon chopped off their arm with his sword."Soon the robbers all ran away and Ammon had protected the king's sheep."

"I'm sure Ammon was very tired after all of this but he wanted to be a good servant and do what he had been told, so he came home and began taking care of the King's horses and chariot. Let's feed the horses some corn so they won't get hungry and wait for the servants to gather all the arms up to bring back to the King." Add corn and cover to allow macaroni and veggies to finish cooking, approximately 8 minutes.

Use the last grab bag while waiting.

Soup will be hot. While dishing up the soup to the children and allowing it to cool, briefly discuss what happened after Ammon returned before the King.

Allow the children to discuss with you their ideas about this story and those they acted out. Help them see how the stories can be examples to them of how Heavenly Father would like us to live.

Bare your testimony of the importance of having scriptures to guide our lives.

Activity:

Materials needed:

* 3 brown paper grocery bags

Nephi and his brothers building a boat—

* Child's plastic tool set
* Towels for fur robes
* Bathtub plastic boat to work on
* Gospel Art Picture #303 "Nephi Subdues His Rebellious Brothers"

Samuel the Lamanite on the city wall—

* Coupon for use of one chair to stand on
* One dozen wadded-up paper balls
* Robe for Samuel
* Gospel Art Picture #314 "Samuel the Lamanite on the Wall"

Alma the Younger sees an angel—

* Brightly colored cloth for robes
* White sheet for angel
* Several pieces of costume jewelry
* Gospel Art Picture #321 "Conversion of Alma the Younger"

Use this lesson to re-enforce:

* *Faith in God*, learning and living the gospel
* *Cub Scouts*, Wolf Achievement 8 and Elective 2, and Bear Achievement 9
* *Gospel Principles*, chapter 10
* *Family Home Evening Resource Book*, lesson 32, and lesson ideas "mission preparation"
* *My Gospel Standards*
* *Primary 2*, lesson 11
* *Primary 3*, lesson 24
* *Primary 4*, lesson 17
* *Book of Mormon Gospel Doctrine Manual*, lessons 1, 25 and 26
* *Aaronic Priesthood 1*, lesson 33
* *Young Women 1*, lesson 27

Fifteen
The Word of Wisdom

Scripture: "And all saints who remember to keep and do these sayings, walking in obedience to the commandments, shall receive health in their navel and marrow to their bones; And shall find wisdom and great treasures of knowledge, even hidden treasures;"
—D&C 89:18-20

Song: "The Lord Gave Me a Temple," *Children's Songbook*, pg. 153.

Treat: Fruit and Vegetable Tray

Lesson:
Materials Needed:
* Chalk and Chalkboard
* Doctrine and Covenants for each child
* Television and video player
* *Family Home Evening Video Supplement* set to "True to the Faith" (9 minutes) or New Testament Video Presentations for Youth and Adult Gospel Doctrine Classes on the segment "The Body Is a Temple" (6 minutes)
* Copies of the section "Physical Health" from the church produced pamphlet *For The Strength of Youth*, 2001

Read D&C 93:33-35. Help the children understand that our bodies and our spirits are sacred and special to Heavenly Father. They are a temple we carry with us where ever we go and can bring us great joy, but only if we learn to keep them clean and healthy.

Label the chalkboard into three sections: Do, Don't and Blessings.

Have the children open their scriptures to D&C 89. Take turns reading these verses. As you go, take notes on the chalkboard about the different things mentioned in the revelation. Let the children draw pictures on the chalkboard to accompany the statements of interest or amusement (bathing with alcohol, sick cows, horses etc.).

Point out verse four especially. Heavenly Father knew that Satan would try his best to get us to defile our bodies. When this revelation was written, many of the things we have now that can be harmful to our bodies and spirits weren't available. Ask the children to name a few things that are not mentioned specifically, but that they know are bad for them. Share that Heavenly Father meant this revelation to be a guide to help us always judge the good from the bad. He didn't need to make a list of every single thing that would ever be bad, if we followed the word of wisdom, we would learn to judge for ourselves.

Play your chosen video segment and review the words on physical health from *For the Strength of Youth.*

Activity:

Materials Needed:

* Old Magazines, both worldly and church oriented, which can be cut up
* 2 pieces of construction paper for each child
* Scissors for each child
* Glue

Allow the children to go through the magazines and cut out pictures that represent good and bad choices. They will divide these choices as learned about in the word of wisdom and glue them into collages on their papers. One paper should represent only good choices, the other only bad.

Use this lesson to re-enforce:

* *Faith in God*, developing talents
* *Family Home Evening Resource Book*, lesson ideas "word of wisdom"
* *My Gospel Standards*
* Cub Scouts, Wolf Achievement 8
* *Primary 3*, lesson 14
* *Primary 5*, lesson 24
* *Primary 6*, lesson 40
* *Aaronic Priesthood 1*, lesson 18
* *Aaronic Priesthood 2*, lesson 27
* *Aaronic Priesthood 3*, lesson 27
* *Young Women 1*, lesson 38
* *Doctrine and Covenants and Church History Gospel Doctrine Manual*, lesson 22
* *For the Strength of Youth*, "Physical Health"

Sixteen
Seek for Knowledge

Scripture: "And as all have not faith, seek ye diligently and teach one another words of wisdom; yea, seek ye out of the best books words of wisdom; seek learning, even by study and by faith."

—D&C 88:118

Song: "Search, Ponder, and Pray," *Children's Songbook*, pg. 109.

Treat: Graham cracker books—have the children put peanut butter between two crackers then use icing tubes to write titles on the outside.

Lesson:
Materials Needed:
* Bible
* Chalkboard and chalk or other writing implements
* Blindfolds for each child
* Paper
* Cardstock
* Drawing and coloring utensils
* Scissors
* Copies of the section "Education" and "Entertainment and The Media" from the church produced pamphlet *For the Strength of Youth*, 2001

Note: prior to this lesson, ask the children to bring one book with them that they have enjoyed reading.

Have each child place a blindfold on, and then ask them to walk from one end of the room to the other. An inside room that can be completely darkened will work as well.

When everyone has covered the distance, ask each to share how easy or difficult it was to make the journey. Explain that the journey was a little easier because they knew where they were when they started. They probably had a good idea what to expect from the journey. Still, it was not as easy as if the lights were left on and there was no blindfold.

We have been sent to earth much the same way. We can't see everything but because we are members of Christ's true church we know why we are here and what we need to do. Review the plan of salvation with the children briefly. Be sure to remind them that we are trying to become like Heavenly Father. Let them spend some time describing what they think Heavenly Father is like.

Share Proverbs 23:12 with the children.

Heavenly Father is very wise and good. To become like Him, we have been told to gain as much knowledge as we can in this life. He has asked us to study hard and try our best in school, to be inquisitive and learn everything we can.

Reading a lot is one of the very best ways we can learn and grow. Have them share the books they brought with them at this point.

Allow them to voice ways that they can try their best in school. Share the above mentioned sections from the pamphlet For the Strength of Youth, when appropriate, during this portion of your discussion with the children.

Ask them to share what they think they want to be when they grow-up. Do they know what is involved in being able to do their chosen profession?

At this age a few children might have definite ideas of what they would like to do with their lives, some may not. It's all right either way. Tell them that though they may not know for sure what they want to do, it's sort of like their blindfold experience. They may not see everything but they do know that they need to try their best and learn and experience many different things. If they do know exactly where they want to go they can focus their efforts on that direct path.

Give them each a paper and drawing utensils. Ask them to draw a picture of themselves in a profession that they are considering.

Give them a piece of cardstock, instruct them to fold it in half from top to bottom then turn it so that the crease is to the left. Then, draw on the outside as if it were a book cover, leaving a generous space for "titles" to be added at a later time.

Help the children affix the picture they drew to the inside of the cardstock cover they created. Tell them this is their goal book, a story of them succeeding in life.

Encourage them to ask several people (parents, teachers, or individuals who have similar careers to those the children have depicted in their books) to tell them what they must study and learn to work in that profession. These are the titles that they should put on the front of their books. You might choose to display these when they are completed or at least let the children share what they learned on a later day.

Activity:

Materials Needed:

* Copies of the symbols and scripture references for each child
* Several sheets of tissue paper
* Colored pencils
* Each child's personal scriptures. If some children do not have their own scriptures try to arrange for them to have a set of their own before this activity, or give them a special three ring binder to collect scripture phrases in. They can then trace and copy the scripture onto plain copier paper and hole-punch them for storage in their notebook.

Show the children that they will be looking up scriptures about learning and knowledge and tracing in the corresponding picture to remind them what the scripture is about. Have them practice using a light touch to trace and color their pictures on tissue paper. Remind them not to press too hard or color darkly or they will tear their pages, or not be able to read the words underneath.

Use this lesson to re-enforce:
* *Faith in God*, "developing talents"
* Cub Scouts, Wolf Elective 6, Bear Achievement 17, and Webelos "Scholar" badge
* *My Gospel Standards*
* *Gospel Principles*, chapter 22
* *Family Home Evening Resource Book*, lesson ideas "learning"
* *Doctrine and Covenants and Church History Gospel Doctrine Manual*, lesson 23
* *Aaronic Priesthood 2*, lesson 33
* *Aaronic Priesthood 3*, lesson 48
* *Young Women Personal Progress*, Faith 12

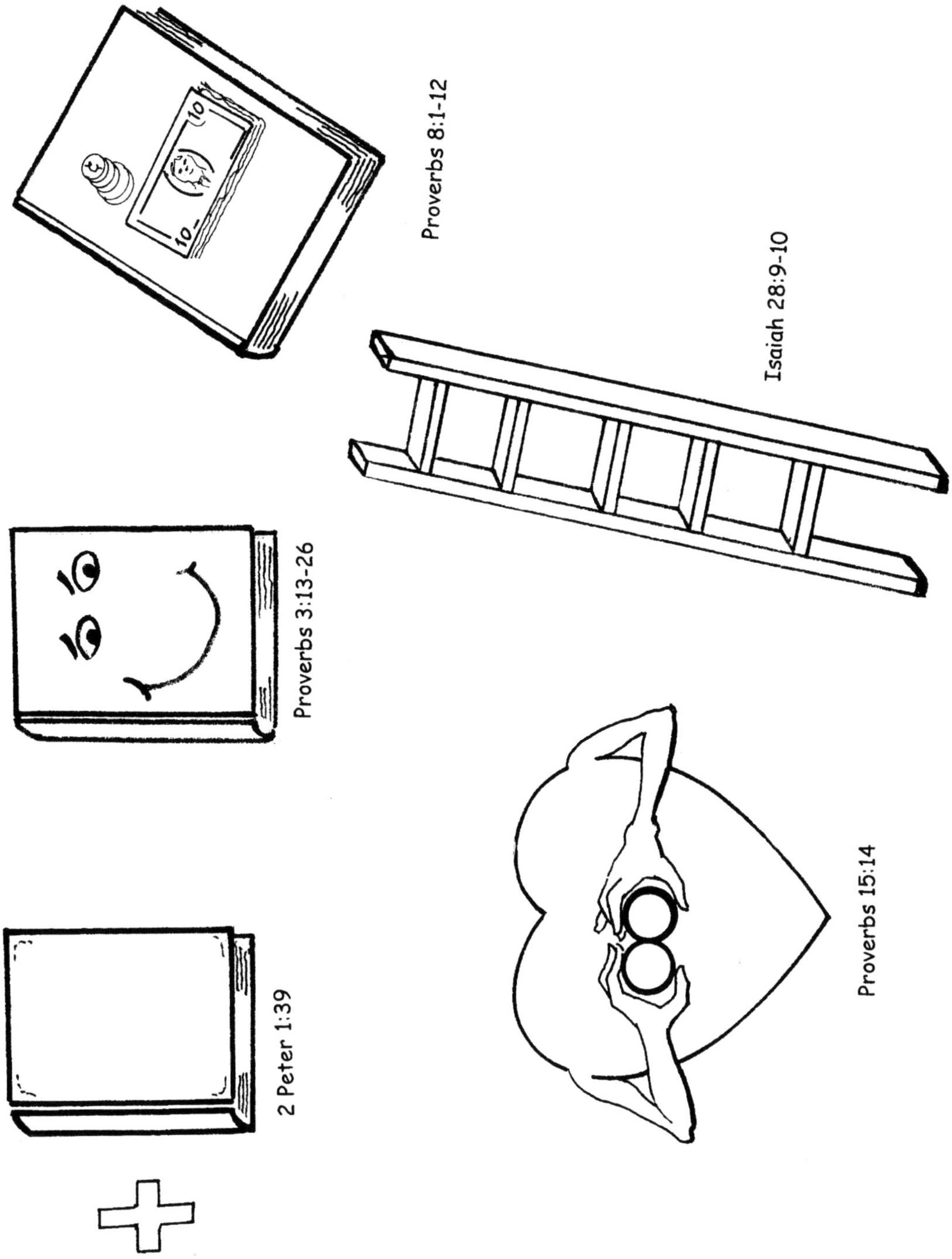
Proverbs 8:1-12
Isaiah 28:9-10
Proverbs 3:13-26
Proverbs 15:14
2 Peter 1:39

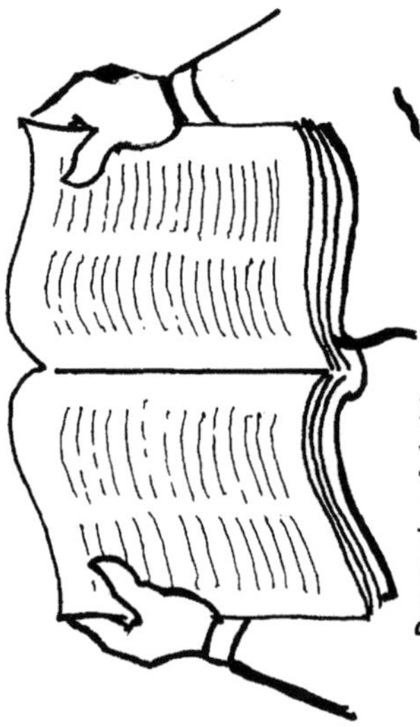

Proverbs 4:1-13

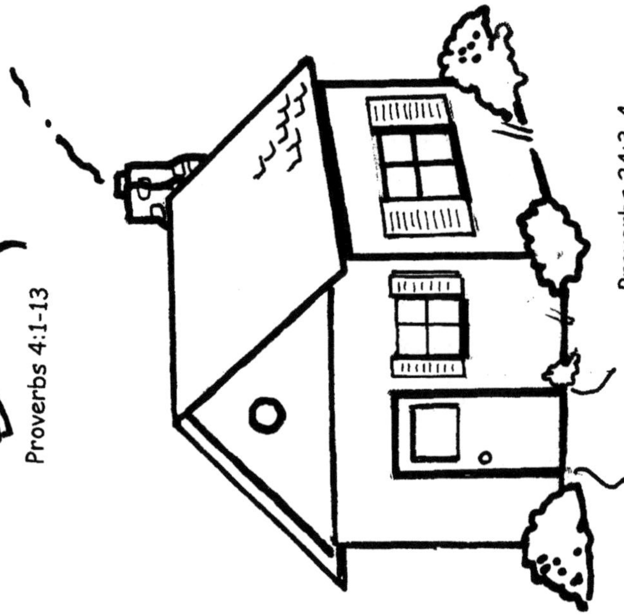

Proverbs 24:3-4

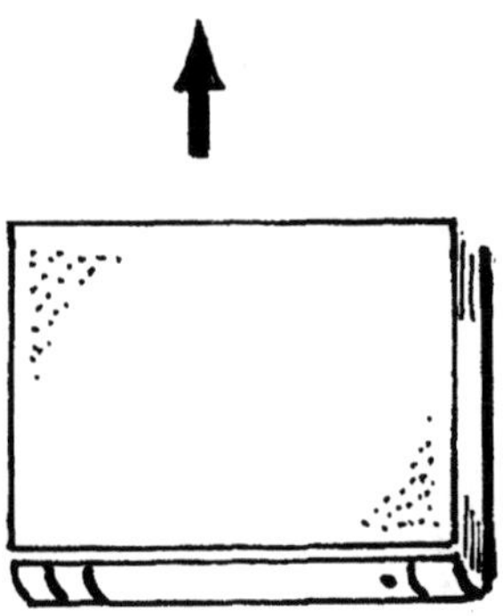

D&C 130:18-19

Proverbs 8:33

Seventeen
Becoming Secret Service Agents

Scripture: "If I then, your Lord and Master, have washed your feet; ye also ought to wash one another's feet. For I have given you an example, that ye should do as I have done to you. Verily, verily, I say unto you, the servant is not greater than his lord; neither he that is sent greater than he that sent him. If ye know these things, happy are ye if ye do them."
—John 13:14-17

Song: "I'm Trying to Be Like Jesus," *Children's Songbook*, pg. 78.

Treat: Hershey® Hugs and Kisses

Lesson:
Materials Needed:
* Bible for each child
* Props for enactment of the story of the good Samaritan—towels and robes, purses of "money," bandages, bedroll for the inn, child's wagon (beast), etc.
* Large handbag or small suitcase with the following items- hammer (hard work), paper heart (love for others), bottle of lotion (gentleness), running shoes (to go the extra mile), binoculars (quietly watching for chances to serve), telephone (listening ear, kind words), scriptures (in tune with the spirit), book (willingness to learn and understand others)
* Copies of the section "Service to Others" from the church produced pamphlet *For the Strength of Youth*, 2001

Review with the children the story found in Luke 10:30-37 (the Good Samaritan), let them act out the story with the props you provided.

Review the "Service to Others" section of the youth pamphlet. Ask the children to share their thoughts and ideas about how they can perform service for those around them and why they should.

Show the children your bag of secret service tools. Name the items and help the children guess what they each represent. Encourage them to look for opportunities to give secret service to those around them. When they do, they'll fill their own spiritual bag with more of the tools of a good agent and will find great happiness in giving service.

Activity:
Materials Needed:
* Notebook and writing utensil, or
* Materials needed to complete an act of secret service

Help the children plan out how to conduct a service project or be prepared to assist them in completing a small assignment this night.

Use this lesson to re-enforce:

* *Faith in God*, "serving others"
* *Gospel Principles*, chapter 28
* Cub Scouts, Wolf Elective 2, and Bear Achievement 24
* *Family Home Evening Resource Book*, lessons 23-26
* *Primary 1*, lessons 22 and 34
* *Aaronic Priesthood 1*, lesson 14
* *Aaronic Priesthood 2*, lesson 6
* *Aaronic Priesthood 3*, lesson 44
* *Young Women 1*, lesson 30
* *Young Women 2*, lesson 30
* *Young Women 3*, lesson 32
* *Doctrine and Covenants and Church History Gospel Doctrine Manual*, lesson 44
* *For the Strength of Youth*, "service to others"

Eighteen
The First Vision

Scripture: "So, in accordance with this, my determination to ask of God, I retired to the woods to make the attempt. It was on the morning of a beautiful, clear day, early in the spring of eighteen hundred and twenty. It was the first time in my life that I had made such an attempt, for amidst all my anxieties I had never as yet made the attempt to pray vocally. It no sooner appeared than I found myself delivered from the enemy which held me bound. When the light rested upon me I saw two Personages, whose brightness and glory defy all description, standing above me, calling me by name and said, pointing to the other—This is My Beloved Son. Hear Him!"

—Joseph Smith-History 1:14, 17

Song: "The Sacred Grove," *Children's Songbook*, pg. 87

Treat: Trees and flowers (broccoli and cauliflower) with dip

Lesson:
Materials Needed:
* Pearl of Great Price or copy of Joseph Smith-History 1:7-20 for each child

Have the children take turns reading the verses containing Joseph Smith's account of the first vision. Help the children recognize the presence of the spirit and encourage them to write their feelings down in their journals and share them, when they share the story with their families.

They will be constructing a diorama as they discuss each part of the vision and practicing telling it so that they can share these things with their own families in a future family home evening. Depending on how quickly the children work, you might plan on using this activity for two nights. The full construction takes anywhere from an hour to an hour and a half.

Activity:
Materials Needed:
* Large shoe box
* Aluminum foil or wire
* Two metal brads (paper fasteners)
* Small light bulb (such as used in a flashlight)
* Electrical tape (preferable, but any tape will work)
* Three small paper clips

* 1 AA battery
* 12x12 piece of green felt
* Miniature silk flowers
* Two brown pipe cleaners
* White craft paper
* Markers, crayons or colored pencils
* Glue
* Scissors

Materials listed are for construction of one diorama, make sure you have enough for each child.

If desired, for a cleaner look: have the children cover the outside of their boxes with craft paper.

Place a small colored book made from craft paper on one end of the lid to the box. Write James 1:5 on the book.

Children will need to cut a small hole (about 3") in one of the long ends of their shoebox; this will be for viewing portions of the story when the lid is on the box.

Begin construction with the light mechanism as this takes the most work. Wire may be used, if available, in the place of the foil strips.

Light Circuit Construction:

1. Poke two small holes in the top of the box, no more than a paper clip width apart. Thread a paper clip onto one of the brads. Insert the metal brads through the lid, so that the button tops and paper clip are on the outside of the lid. Spread the clasps apart to hold them in place.

2. Give each child three strips of aluminum foil that are about 1 inch wide. Have them fold it in half length-wise, shiny side out, again and again until the foil is sturdy and no wider than the metal band around their light bulb (about 1/8 inch).

3. Cut a 1 1/2 inch length of tape and place one strip of foil along most of the tape. Carefully have the children wrap the foil around the metal band of their light bulb so that the two metals make contact all the way around the base of the bulb. Use the tape to secure it into position. Snip any extra tape off of the end of the bulb so that the small metal tip is exposed. Fold the free end of the foil into a paper clip.

4. Use another small piece of tape to secure a strip of foil to the small tip of metal on the bottom of the bulb. Secure the free end of this strip to one of the contact points on the battery with a piece of tape.

5. Use the third strip of foil on the other end of the battery. Place a paper clip on the free end. Tuck each paper clip under the end of a metal brad.

6. Tape everything into place as shown in the diagram. Make sure the strips of foil do not touch each other or they will short the circuit out and your bulb will not light.

Connecting the circuit on the outside of the box activates the light. Simply rotate the paper clip so that it touches the other metal brad. This can be safely done with anyone's finger.

Diorama Construction:

1. Measure and cut the craft paper to line the inside of the box on two long and one short side. Then color this piece of paper to depict trees in a forest setting. Glue the picture to the inside of their box, leaving the small side with the cut opening free.

2. Measure and cut a piece of green felt to cover the inside bottom of their box. Glue it into place. This is the grass in their forest clearing. Have them glue small flowers on to the "grass."

3. Next the children will need to create a pipe cleaner Joseph. This requires 1 whole pipe cleaner and 1 half piece of pipe cleaner. Bend the middle of the whole pipe cleaner over a finger to form a loop for the head. Twist the free ends together on the underside of your finger. This makes the neck and shoulders. Place the small piece of pipe cleaner just below the twist (this is your arms) and continue twisting the long pipe cleaner downward. Stop twisting when two-thirds of the cleaner is intertwined. The free portions are the legs. Spread these apart and bend them onto their "knees," counter-balance your figurine by bending the arms in front so that arms appear to be folded. Adjust the figure until it can kneel with stability.

When the child tells the story of the first vision, they will place the figure into the forest box to show Joseph "retired to the woods to make the attempt."

Placing the lid on the box represents darkness descending; the scene can still be viewed through the small opening in one end.

The child will connect the light to dispel the darkness with the arrival of Heavenly Father and Jesus. The rest of the story is told with out the use of the diorama.

Use this lesson to re-enforce:

* *Faith in God*, "learning and living the gospel" and "developing talents"
* Cub Scouts, Webelos "engineer" badge
* *Family Home Evening Resource Book*, lesson 7
* *My Gospel Standards*
* *Primary 1*, lesson 2
* *Primary 3*, lesson 5
* *Primary 5*, lesson 1

Parts List for First Vision Diorama

AA Battery
(power source)

Tinfoil Strips* or Wire (3)
(**conductor**)

* See directions for how to make these

Electrical Tape
made of rubber (**insulator**)

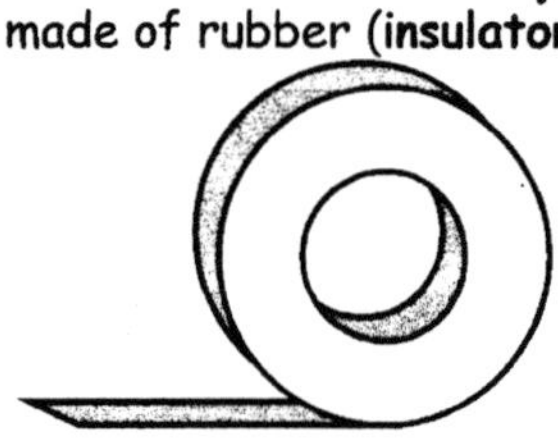

Light Bulb
(1.5 Volt) or Single Cell

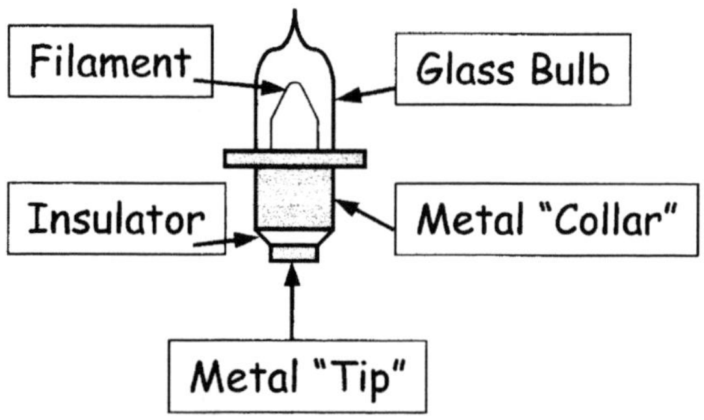

Paper Clips (5)
(**conductor**)

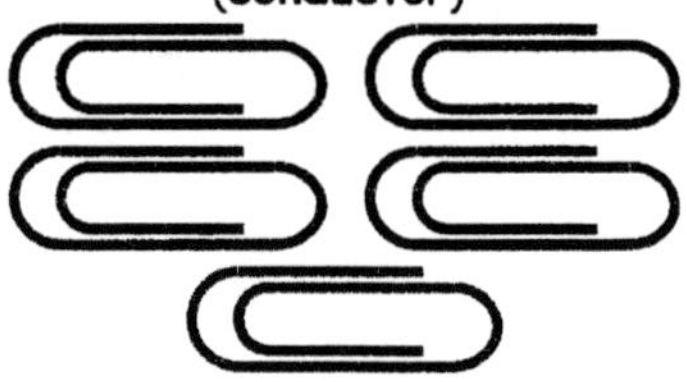

Brads (2)
sometimes called "Paper Fasteners"
made of metal (**conductor**)

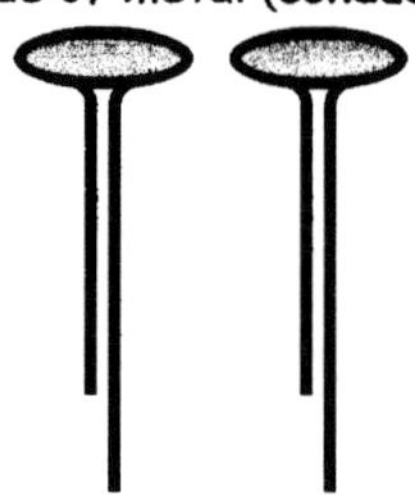

Shoe Box (with lid)
(**conductor**)

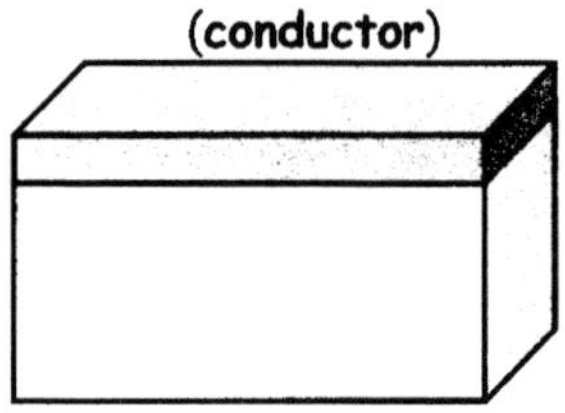

First Vision Diorama
Light and Battery Preparation

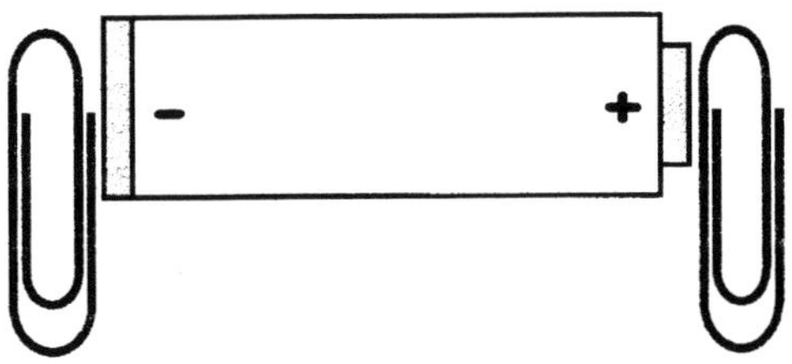

Place the paperclips flat on the ends of the battery.
Make sure that one end of each paperclip is sticking out. (see diagram)
Tape the paperclips in place.
(run the tape several times around the battery from end to end)

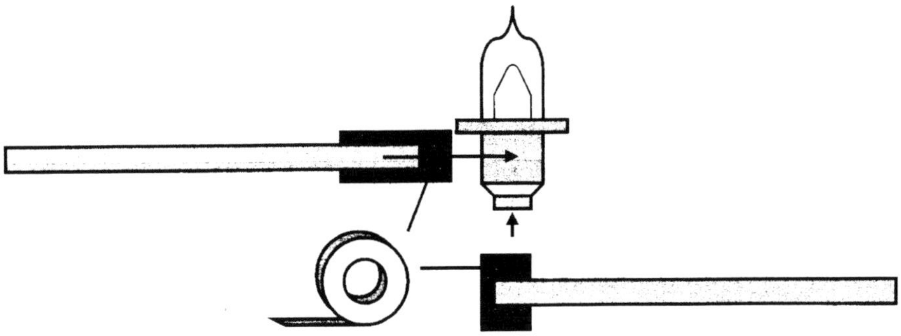

Place a short piece of tape on one end of the tinfoil strips (or wire).
Wrap the tape around the metal collar of the light bulb.
IMPORTANT!!
Make sure that some of the tinfoil strip (or wire) touches the metal collar.

Tape one end of the other tinfoil strip (or wire) to the metal tip of the light bulb.
IMPORTANT!!
Make sure that the tinfoil strip on the tip does not touch the collar and that the collar strip doesn't touch the tip.

Do not put tape on the glass part of the light bulb.

First Vision Diorama Assembly Diagram

Top of Box Lid

Underside of Box Lid

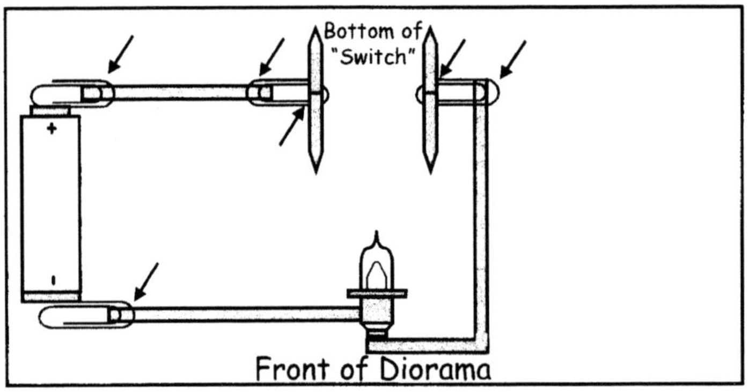

Tape the battery and light securely to the inside of the box lid.

Tape everything the arrow points at to the top of the box.

Note: Clamp the paperclips around the tinfoil strips (or wire)for the best connection possible and then tape over the connection to hold it in place.

Nineteen
So, You're an Artist

Scripture: "And all this for the benefit of the church of the living God, that every man may improve upon his talent, that every man may gain other talents, yea, even an hundred fold . . ."

—D&C 82:18

Song: "Our Primary Colors," *Children's Songbook*, pg. 258.

Treat: Bread dough sculptures

Lesson:
Materials Needed:
* Pictures of artwork by the selected artists you will be featuring in your activity. Available on the internet for printing, or in book form at you local libraries.

Briefly discuss with the children the blessings that come from discovering and using talents. Explain that Heavenly Father is pleased with us for trying new things and adding beauty to our surroundings. Share the pictures you brought, and tell the children something about the artist and how they worked. This will make instruction time less during the activities. Use most of the time to allow the children hands-on experiences with different modes of artistic expression.

Activity:
Materials Needed:
* Marking pen to label children's work

Listed below is the name of an artist, a brief biography and the materials needed to allow the children to try producing artwork in the same style. Plan on having the children wear old clothes, provide newspaper or other protection for the tables and floor and have plenty of workspace available.

August Rodin (1840-1917) - Had to study for many years before he was recognized as an accomplished sculptor. He liked to sculpt people and animals as they really appeared, not perfect.

* Prepared bread dough, firm enough for the children to handle and keep its shape. Recipes are widely available in children's cookbooks and on the internet.

Have each child create a bread dough sculpture and place them in the oven to bake, according to recipe instructions, while they are working on the rest of their master pieces.

Michelangelo Buonarroti (1475-1564) - Italian painter and sculptor. He preferred sculpting, but people mostly paid him to paint. It took him four years to paint the ceiling of the Sistine Chapel lying down on his back.

* Washable tempera paints
* Tape
* Paper
* Paintbrushes
* Water for rinsing brushes

Tape your paper under a low table or chair and try to paint a picture lying down.

Gustave Courbet (1819-1877) - His family sent him to Paris to become a lawyer; he decided to be a painter instead. He liked to use a knife to spread his paint onto the canvas because he liked the different textures it could make.

* Plastic knives or popsicle sticks
* Acrylic paints or tempera paints that have been thickened with flour, corn starch or other thickener
* Cardstock quality paper

Have the children try and "butter" their paper and create a picture.

Alexander Calder (1889-1976) - Calder trained as a design engineer. He was most famous for creating the style of art known as "mobile" or art that moves.

* Craft wire
* Craft scissors
* Blocks of Styrofoam™
* Glue
* Paper Scissors
* Bits of colored paper and strings

The children are to cut and place lengths of wire into the Styrofoam™ then glue paper and strings to it: bending and shaping the wires as desired.

Pablo Picasso (1881-1973) - He is one of the most famous artists. He worked in a style called "cubism." This meant that most of his work looked like a bunch of square and triangular pieces of a puzzle put together wrong.

* Drawing paper
* Construction paper
* Drawing utensils
* Scissors
* Glue

Have the children draw a picture, then cut it into large pieces. Then let them glue the pieces onto the construction paper, rearranging their placement and orientation slightly.

Marcel Duchamp (1887-1968) - He was a painter who prided himself on being a "free-thinker" some of his most famous works were what he termed "happy accidents."

* Bits of string or yarn approximately 6"-12" long
* Dishes of washable tempera paint
* Large sheets of paper

Have the children carefully dip strings into the various colors of paint. Then drop (or drag) them from above onto their papers, and then carefully remove it, to make different designs.

Use this lesson to re-enforce:

* *Faith in God*, developing talents
* *Family Home Evening Resource Book*, lesson ideas "talents and gifts"
* Cub Scouts, Wolf Elective 12, Bear Elective 9, Webelos "artist" badge
* *Gospel Principles*, chapter 34
* *Primary 2*, lesson 35
* *Primary 7*, lesson 26
* *Young Women 1*, lesson 47
* *Young Women 2*, lesson 45

Twenty
On Our Best Behavior

Scripture: "And as ye would that men should do to you, do ye also to them likewise."
—St. Luke 6:31

Song: "A Special Gift Is Kindness," *Children's Songbook*, pg. 145.

Treat: Perfect Kids—gingerbread boys (or girls)

Lesson:
Materials Needed:
* Pencil and Paper
* Materials to make invitations
* Full place setting
* Stop watch or watch with second hand

Help the children plan a dinner for their parents. They should help cook a simple meal, formally invite their parents, plan a seating arrangement and table settings, and display their best manners during the meal. Review how they should act in a dinner situation and what will be expected of them.

Show them how to properly set a table, and then time each child to see how quickly they can set a table.

Let them make invitations when the date and time and other details have been set. Make sure that you allow enough time before and after for the children to be involved in preparation and clean-up from this parent-child event.

Activity:
Materials Needed:
* Chalkboard and Chalk
* Slips of paper with different etiquette tips listed on them

Play "Pictionary" with manners. The children take turns choosing a situation then drawing it to see if the rest of the children can guess what it means. With each situation, be sure to take a minute to review what the proper behavior would be.

Situations could include:
* Keep your elbows off the table
* Your napkin goes in your lap
* Ask for things to be passed to you when they're out of easy reach

* Open doors for your elders
* Take a lady's arm to escort her
* Know which utensils to use and when
* Introduce your guests to each other
* What do you do with food you don't like
* How to talk to someone on the phone
* Your invited to a party you can't attend

Recommended Books on Manners:

* *365 Manners Kids Should Know: Games, Activities and Other Fun Ways to Help Children Learn Etiquette* by Sheryl Eberly
* *How Rude!: The Teenager's Guide to Good Manners, Proper Behavior, and Not Grossing People Out* by Alex J. Packer, et al.

Use this lesson to re-enforce:

* *Faith in God*, serving others
* *Family Home Evening Resource Book*, lesson ideas "manners"
* *My Gospel Standards*
* Cub Scouts, Wolf Achievement 8 and Elective 9, and Bear Achievements 9 and 18d
* *Aaronic Priesthood 2*, lesson 23
* *Young Women 1*, lesson 31
* *Young Women 2*, lesson 19

Twenty-one
The Word Jungle

Scripture: "And by them their children were taught to read and write, having a language which was pure and undefiled."

—Moses 6:6

Song: "Hum Your Favorite Hymn," *Children's Songbook*, pg. 152.

Treat: Letters on a log—spread peanut butter in celery sticks and provide an alphabet cereal to stick in the peanut butter and form words.

Lesson:
Materials Needed:
* Copies of the section "Language" from the church produced pamphlet *For the Strength of Youth*, 2001
* Several poetry books for young children from your local library
* Paper and pencil for each child
* Chalkboard and chalk

Tell the children that Heavenly Father has given each of us wonderful, creative and quick-thinking minds. The more we use them, the more we grow and learn. Ask them if they have any habits, such as biting their nails or always saying the same things when they pray.

Sometimes we develop habits because we don't really think about what we are doing every time we do it. The habit of swearing is one of those things. We have learned by listening to others that there are certain words most people tend to use when their angry or annoyed or at other times.

We hear them a lot, even when we try not to. Then one day we get mad and without thinking we use the same words. Heavenly Father has asked us to keep our language clean and avoid those words that cause bad feelings and make the spirit leave us. That's why it's good to have creativity.

If you stop and think before you speak you can say what you really mean, not what the world tells you to say. If you think of something new and different each time, you feel better because it's fun! It also makes you think of something other than what you're mad at and the spirit can stay with you to help you. Help the children think of some silly phrases they can use instead of reverting to habits that can be crude and insulting.

Read over the statement on language from the pamphlet with the children.

Language is a wonderful thing that can be used to express every human emotion and every thing of beauty. The more we use it, the more we enjoy it. Ask the children to share a favorite story or book that they have enjoyed.

Let the children spend some time looking through the poetry books then have them share something they found that they liked. Show them that the poems can be written in many ways, there are shape poems, rhyming poems, non-sense poems, story poems and many more types.

Play a rhyming game by saying a word and have each of the children see if they can think of a word that rhymes with it. Go around several times.

Have the children choose a topic to make a shape poem. List their ideas about the topic on one side of the chalkboard. Then help them arrange their thoughts into a suitable shape.

Next let them choose their own gospel topic and let them try writing a poem or story on paper about it. Offer individual help and encouragement as they work. Encourage them to take their work home and continue to practice. You might consider posting their finished compositions somewhere to share them with others or creating a small book for each child with all of their work in it.

Recommended poetry books:

* *The Random House Book of Poetry for Children* by Jack Prelutsky and Arnold Lobel
* *A Light in the Attic* by Shel Silverstein
* *An Illustrated Treasury of Read-Aloud Poems for Young People* by Glorya Hale
* *Alligator Pie* by Dennis Lee and Frank Newfield
* *A Child's Garden of Verses* by Robert Stevenson
* *Kids Pick the Funniest Poems: Poems That Make Kids Laugh* by Bruce Lansky.

Activity:

Materials Needed:

* Old magazines
* Scissors for each child
* Glue
* Index cards
* Tape
* Large playing area
* Paper and pencil

Use the tape to mark a start and finish line for a relay race. Have each child cut out 5 different words from the magazines and glue them each to an index card. Then spread them out just beyond the finish line.

Divide the children into two teams, line them up behind the starting line and place a pencil and paper beside the lines. On your mark each person is to run up to the finish line, choose a word and bring it back to the starting line. They tag the next child in line that runs forward after a word and so on. When every child has a word the team must compose a collective poem or story using the words they have chosen (other words can be used as well, but all of the chosen ones must be included). The first team to complete their composition wins.

Use this lesson to re-enforce:

* *Faith in God*, developing talents
* *Family Home Evening Resource Book*, lesson ideas "profanity"
* *My Gospel Standards*
* *For the Strength of Youth*, "Language"
* *Aaronic Priesthood 2*, lesson 47
* *Aaronic Priesthood 3*, lesson 43

Twenty-two
The Money Tree

Scripture: "He also that had received two talents came and said, Lord, thou deliveredst unto me two talents: behold, I have gained two other talents beside them. His lord said unto him, Well done, good and faithful servant; thou hast been faithful over a few things, I will make thee ruler over many things: enter thou into the joy of thy Lord."

—St. Matthew 25:22-23

Song: "The Wise Man and the Foolish Man," *Children's Songbook*, pg. 281.

Treat: Cake baked in 8x11 pan iced and decorated to look like a dollar bill

Lesson:

Materials Needed:

* Large poster board
* Paints, markers or other method to decorate poster
* Brown yarn
* Scissors
* Green construction paper
* Writing pen
* Chalkboard and chalk or dry erase board
* Tape

Prior to the meeting: draw and color a large tree on the poster board.

Cut the construction paper into 2 1/2 inches by 6 inch strips.

Write the situations on each piece of construction paper then fold them length-wise accordion style.

Cut 6 inch strands of yarn then use the scissors to randomly punch pairs of holes into the branches of the tree. Thread the two free ends of your pieces of yarn through each pair of holes from the back, and then use the yarn to tie your "bills" to the tree.

Make two columns on the chalkboard: wise and foolish.

The children will take turns picking money off of the money tree and seeing if the situation written on it is a wise or foolish use of money. When their decision is made, tape the paper under the correct column.

Possible situations:

* You pay your tithing before you do anything else with your money.
* You spent your week's lunch money on a new CD.

* You have already started saving for your mission.
* You have been saving to buy a new pair of jeans you want.
* You borrowed money from your sister to go to the movies.
* You got your allowance Monday, its Wednesday, it's gone and you don't know where it went.
* You went shopping today and decided to buy yourself ten candy bars.
* You gave a dollar to a man collecting money for the poor.
* You bought a pair of tennis shoes that were on sale instead of paying twice as much for the "cooler" pair.
* You try to take care of your things so they last longer.
* You do odd jobs to earn extra money instead of begging for a raise in your allowance.

Activity:

Materials Needed:

* Wallpaper or heavy card stock
* Scissors
* Several copies of the instructions
* Stapler
* Markers

Help each child construct three origami boxes to use as a bank. Staple the boxes in a row and label the fronts: tithing, savings and fun.

Special notes:

1. Begin with a square of paper that is 8 to 12 inches wide.
2. If using a patterned paper, begin with the patterned or dominate side facing down.

Use this lesson to re-enforce:

* *Faith in God*, developing talents
* *Family Home Evening Resource Book*, lesson ideas "money management" and "tithing"
* Cub Scouts, Bear Achievement 13, and Webelos "family member" badge
* *Primary 3*, lesson 42
* *Young Women 2*, lesson 46
* *Young Women 3*, lesson 46

1. Fold along the diagonals and then open back up.

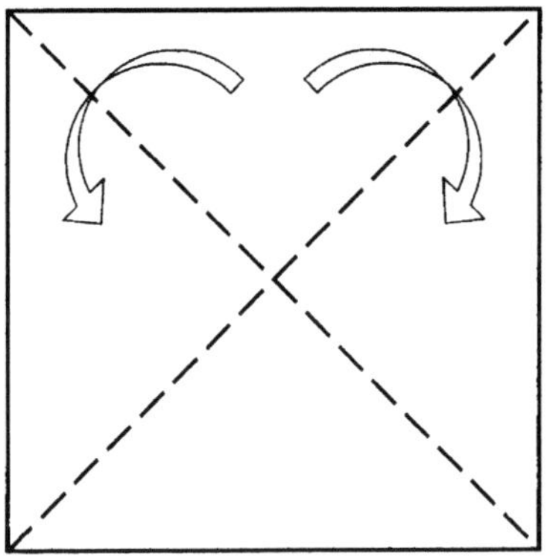

2. Fold the corners into the center.

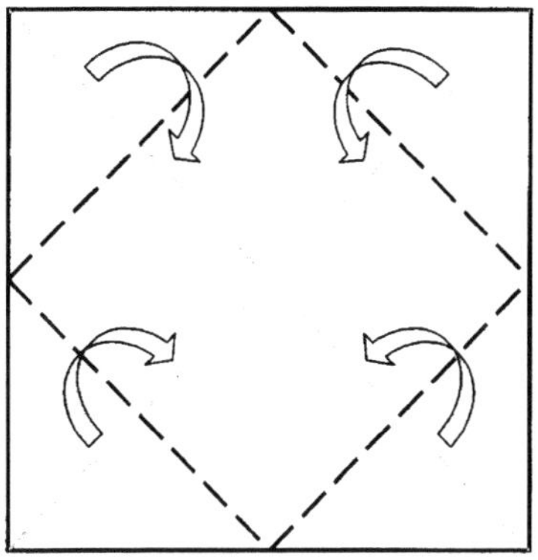

3. Rotate the paper until it looks like a square.

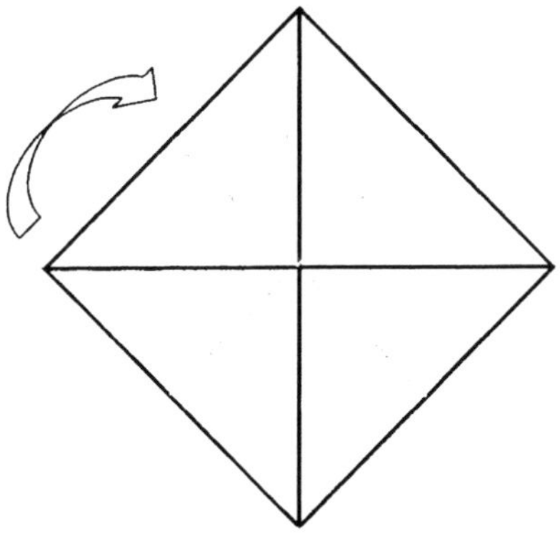

4. Unfold one flap.

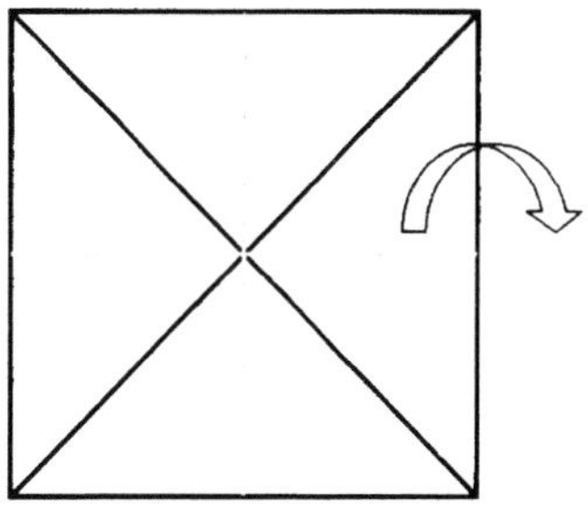

5. Fold the open flap in half until the corner reaches the crease.

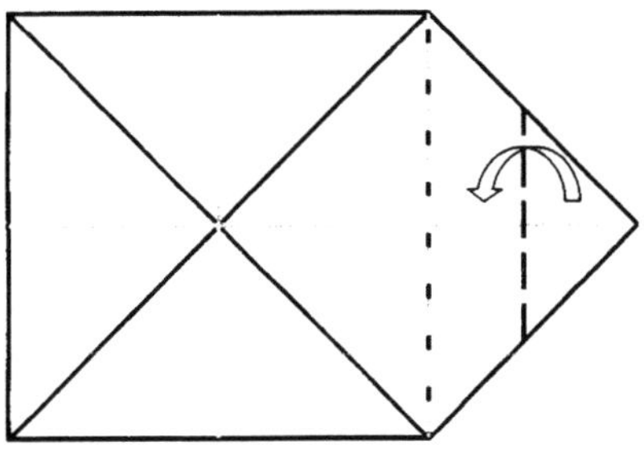

6. Fold the flap back in.

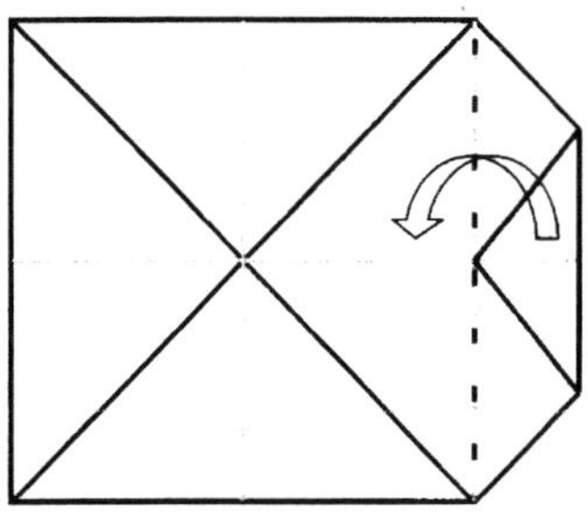

7. Repeat steps 4. through 6. with the other three flaps.

8. Your paper should look like this. Now flip it completely over.

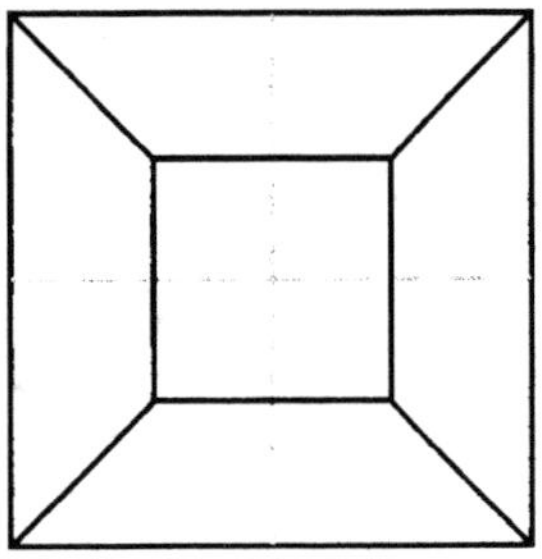

9. Fold the top and bottom until they touch the center crease. Open back up.

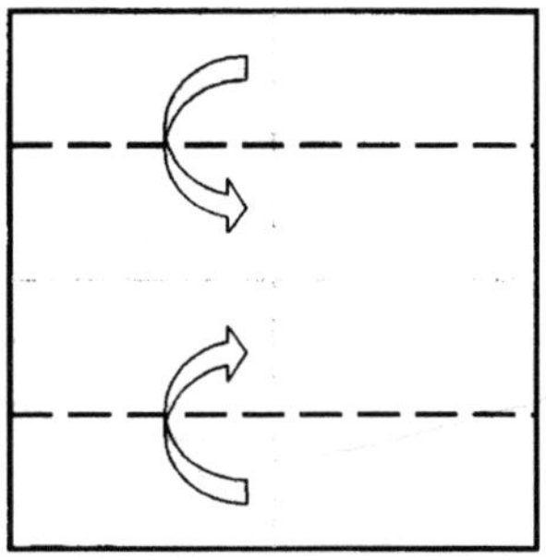

10. Fold the right and left edges in until they touch the center crease.

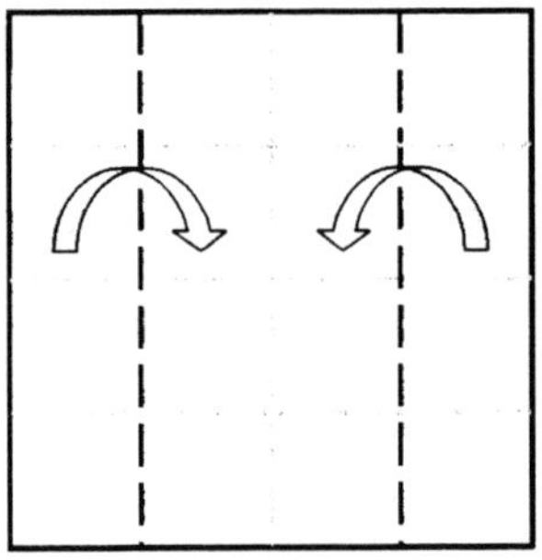

11. Unfold the topmost flap only.

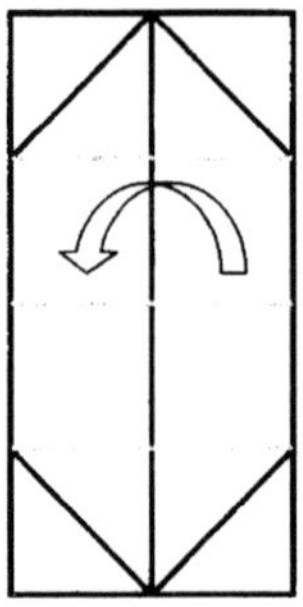

12. Fold the top and bottom corners in until they reach the center crease.

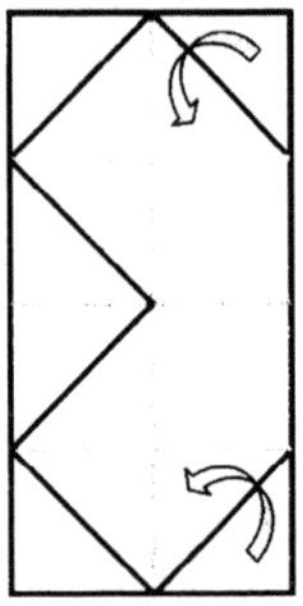

13. Fold the topmost flap back.

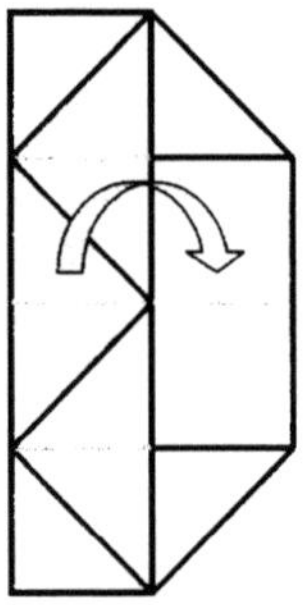

14. Repeat steps 11. through 13. with the left flap.

15. Your paper should look like this.

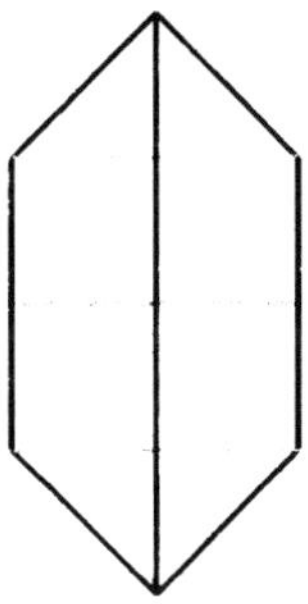

16. Gently pull the center edges outward. This will cause the top and bottom to move towards the center.

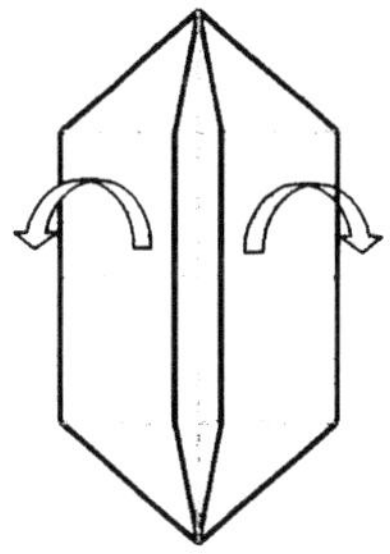

16. Continue to open the box by pulling the right and left edges until they are straight up

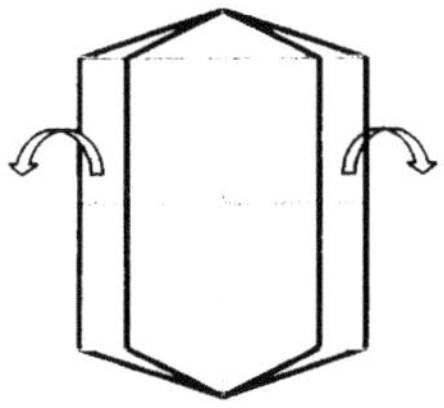

17. Finish the box by shaping the sides until they are all upright.

18. Your finished box should look like this.

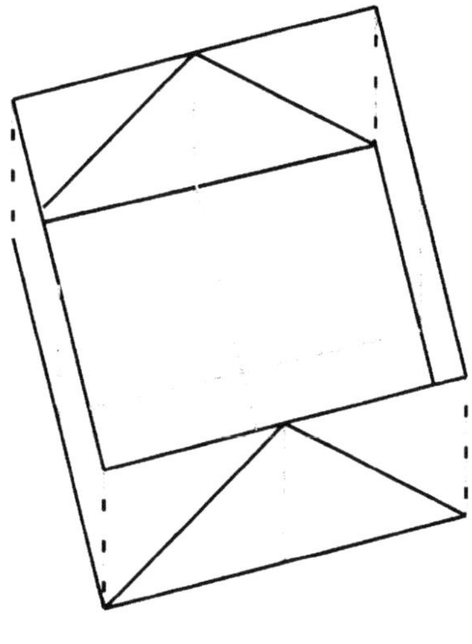

Twenty-three
I've Got Rhythm!

Scripture: " If thou art merry, praise the Lord with singing, with music, with dancing, and with a prayer of praise and thanksgiving."

—D&C 136:28

Song: "We'll Bring the World His Truth," *Children's Songbook*, pg. 172.

Treat: Drum Sticks

Lesson:

Materials Needed:

* Piano/Pianist or recording of "We'll Bring the World His Truth," *Children's Songbook*, pg. 172
* Copy of the above sheet music for each child to look at

Tell the children that they are going to learn lots of ways to enjoy this song.

Introduce the melody to this song by having the piano play while the children try to find the basic rhythm and clap along. You are not looking for perfection, only for them to notice that there is a basic pattern called a beat. Help them sing along with the music while the once again try to clap or march to the beat.

Show the children music you have prepared point out that the lines of music are divided into boxes. Slowly sing the first line of music again as they clap. Can they tell how many times they clapped for the words in each box?

These boxes represent part of the time signature that they see at the beginning of the music. The top number tells us that each box of music will always have three beats (or claps) in it. They can begin counting with one at the start of each box and will reach three by the end of the box. Play several lines of the music again and help them practice clapping and counting "one-two-three" at a steady pace. Can they clap louder with each "one" beat?

Tell them that keeping that steady pace while people are singing or playing music is the job of a chorister or conductor. That's what they are doing when they wave they're arms. They are actually drawing patterns that tell the people how many counts are in each of the boxes on the music and how fast it should be sung.

The pattern a chorister draws for three counts is just like a big triangle. It has three sides; each side gets one count so each time the chorister finishes drawing a triangle you start singing the next box of music. Help them try drawing a triangle in the air while they keep the steady pace they have practiced for counting "one-two-three." Have them experiment setting a slower and faster pace while they sing along.

Sing through the song, with a different child practicing the part of the chorister, until everyone has had a chance to try directing the music and the children are comfortable with the words.

Activity:

Materials Needed:

* Variety of supplies to make simple percussion instruments

Allow the children to construct an instrument that can be used to keep the rhythm in another manner. Then add these to your musical practice of this song. Children can rotate between conducting, clapping, marching, using their instrument and moving their bodies to the different counts as you continue to sing this song.

You may also choose to experiment with other songs from the Children's Songbook that have consistent recognizable beat patterns. Remember to stick with songs written in 3/4 time, or teach them to draw boxes (instead of triangles) and count to four if using a song in 4/4 time.

Emphasize that all of the children must pay attention to the chorister's beat pattern to determine how fast or slow they should go. If they don't - chaos will result.

"Child's play" percussion instruments:

* Fill plastic Easter eggs half-full with rice and super-glue them closed.
* Take 2 plastic or paper plates, hold together and hole punch through the outer rim at 1/4 inch intervals all the way around, place a few beans inside one plate top with the other and whip-stitch it closed with yarn. (Hint: place a drop of glue over the knots in the yarn so children can't open the shaker and take out the beans.) The plates can be colored or other-wise decorated on the outside.
* Use foam or plastic cups, punch holes around rims, place beans in the bottom of one cup, place another cup on top and whip-stitch it closed with yarn. (Hint: place a drop of glue over the knots in the yarn so children can't open the shaker and take out the beans.) These can be colored or other-wise decorated on the outside.
* Cut the top 3 inches off a balloon, stretch it over a plastic cup and secure with a tight rubber band around the rim.
* Any empty container with a sealing lid such as: whip topping, oatmeal and butter containers can be used as drums.
* Wooden spoons and pencils can be used as rhythm sticks.
* Use your imagination! Almost anything you can hit or shake can be used.

Use this lesson to re-enforce:

* *Faith in God*, developing talents
* *Family Home Evening Resource Book*, lesson ideas "music," and family activities "appreciating music"
* *My Gospel Standards*
* *Primary 1*, lesson 39

* *Primary 5*, lesson 14
* *For the Strength of Youth*, "Music and Dancing"
* *Young Women 2*, lesson 45

Index

About the Author

Alison Palmer is a life-long member of the Church. Born in Mesa, Arizona, she grew up in West Virginia and graduated from Marshall University with a Bachelors degree in Nursing. Alison stopped practicing nursing after several years to raise and home school her children.

Over the years, Alison has held many callings in the church, including several that have helped develop her great love for the Primary children. She has served as nursery leader, pianist, chorister, teacher, den leader and Primary President. She has also been spotted teaching Sunday School, serving as a teacher or leader in Relief Society and occasionally braving girl's camp.

Writing is Alison's favorite pastime, but you can also find her lost within the pages of a good book, sewing, cooking, attending the temple, taking long walks or playing with her family. Alison's greatest accomplishments come from the dynamic rewards of raising children who are trying to live righteously.

The Palmers currently reside in Grand Blanc, Michigan.